Find Calm in the Garden of Paradise

ELIZABETH ELIUK

Find Calm in the Garden of Paradise

ISBN 978-1974525737

Also by Elizabeth Eliuk:

Tapestry of Florals: an artist's perspective
ISBN 978-1539917427 • www.CreateSpace.com/6694433

Five-star reviews at Amazon:

★★★★★ "Very well organized and absolutely beautiful! The designs are very ornate, detailed, and
lots of fun coloring these beautiful designs." —*kstars*

★★★★★ "This is a beautiful coloring book. One of the best ones that I have ever colored!" —*a*

Watch for Elizabeth Eliuk's Christmas-themed colouring book,
to be published in the autumn of 2017.

Graphic design by Ingénieuse Productions
Edmonton, Alberta, Canada

Find Calm
in the
Garden of Paradise

*To colour your own tapestry
and create your own
stress-free perspective*

Elizabeth Eliuk

www.facebook.com/people/Elizabeth-Eliuk/100011777359791

www.artwanted.com/artist.cfm?ArtID=85552

www.amazon.com/Elizabeth-Eliuk/e/B073KXLCJB/

BLOGS
dashingdiva.blog
diva9775.wordpress.com

TAPESTRY: AN ARTIST'S PERSPECTIVE
www.facebook.com/emeliuk.art

E-MAIL
eliuk.elizabeth@gmail.com

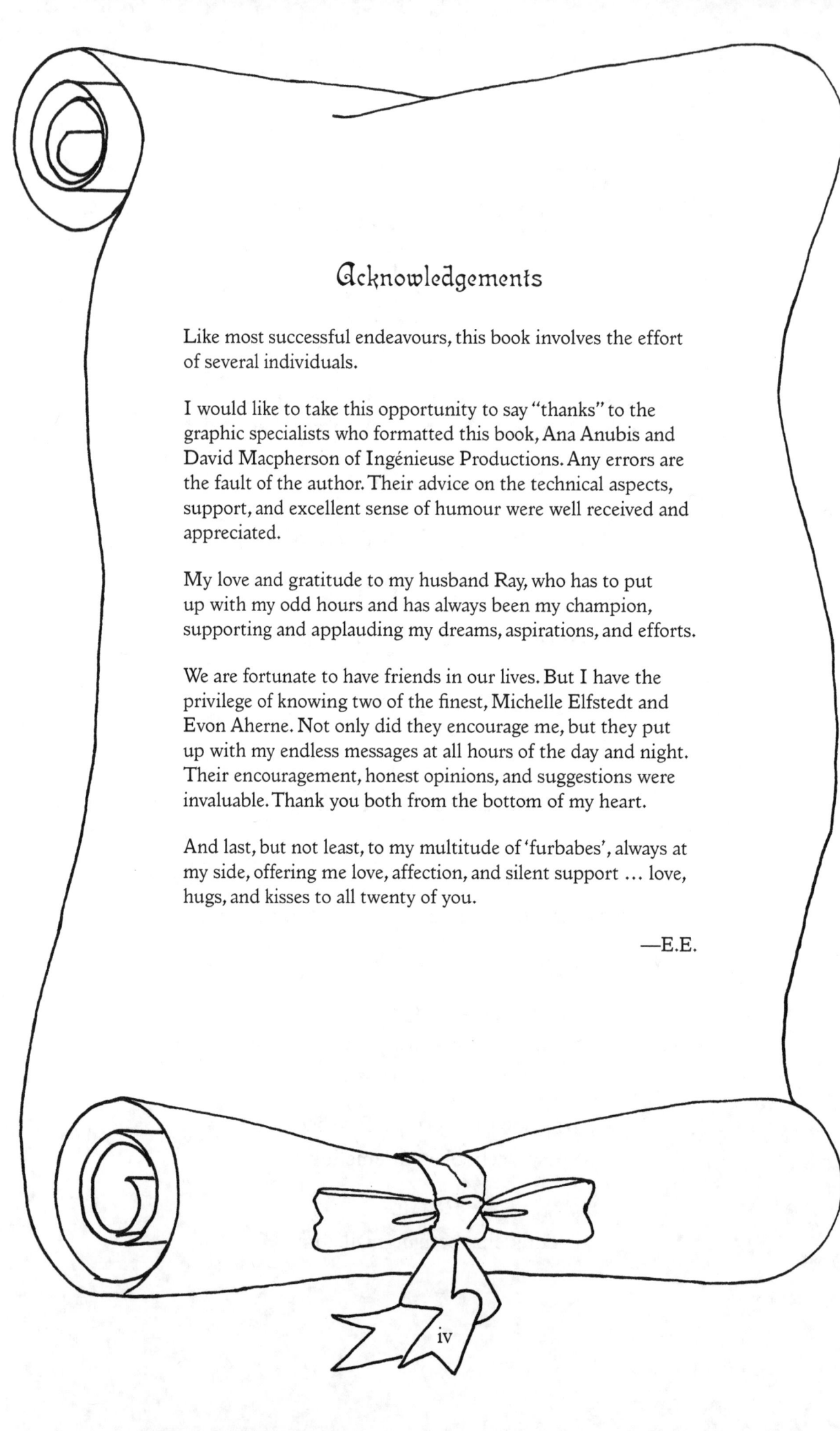

Acknowledgements

Like most successful endeavours, this book involves the effort of several individuals.

I would like to take this opportunity to say "thanks" to the graphic specialists who formatted this book, Ana Anubis and David Macpherson of Ingénieuse Productions. Any errors are the fault of the author. Their advice on the technical aspects, support, and excellent sense of humour were well received and appreciated.

My love and gratitude to my husband Ray, who has to put up with my odd hours and has always been my champion, supporting and applauding my dreams, aspirations, and efforts.

We are fortunate to have friends in our lives. But I have the privilege of knowing two of the finest, Michelle Elfstedt and Evon Aherne. Not only did they encourage me, but they put up with my endless messages at all hours of the day and night. Their encouragement, honest opinions, and suggestions were invaluable. Thank you both from the bottom of my heart.

And last, but not least, to my multitude of 'furbabes', always at my side, offering me love, affection, and silent support … love, hugs, and kisses to all twenty of you.

—E.E.

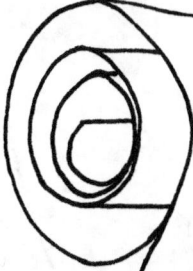

Contents

DESIGNS

The title of each design is indicative of the content in the image, which reflects William Morris's style of naming his work.

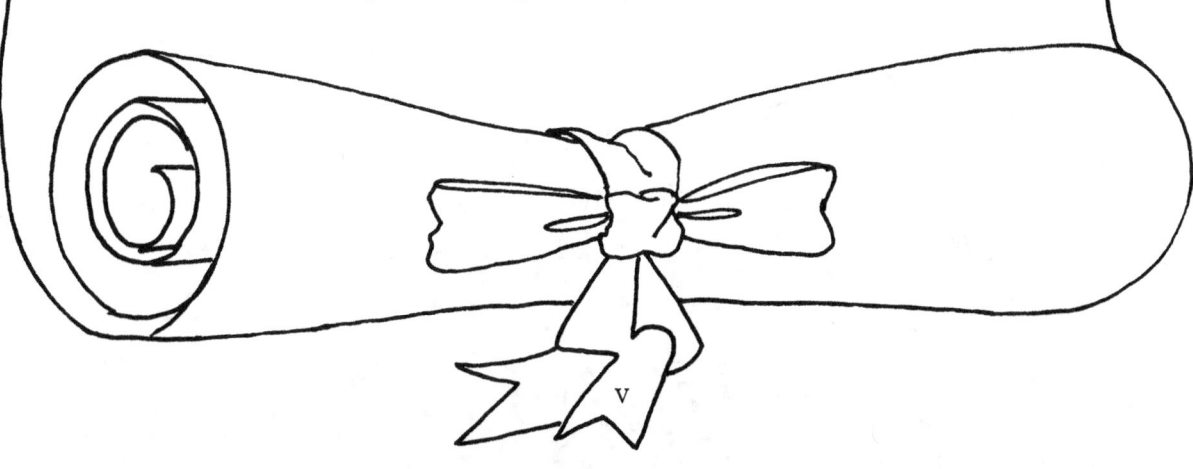

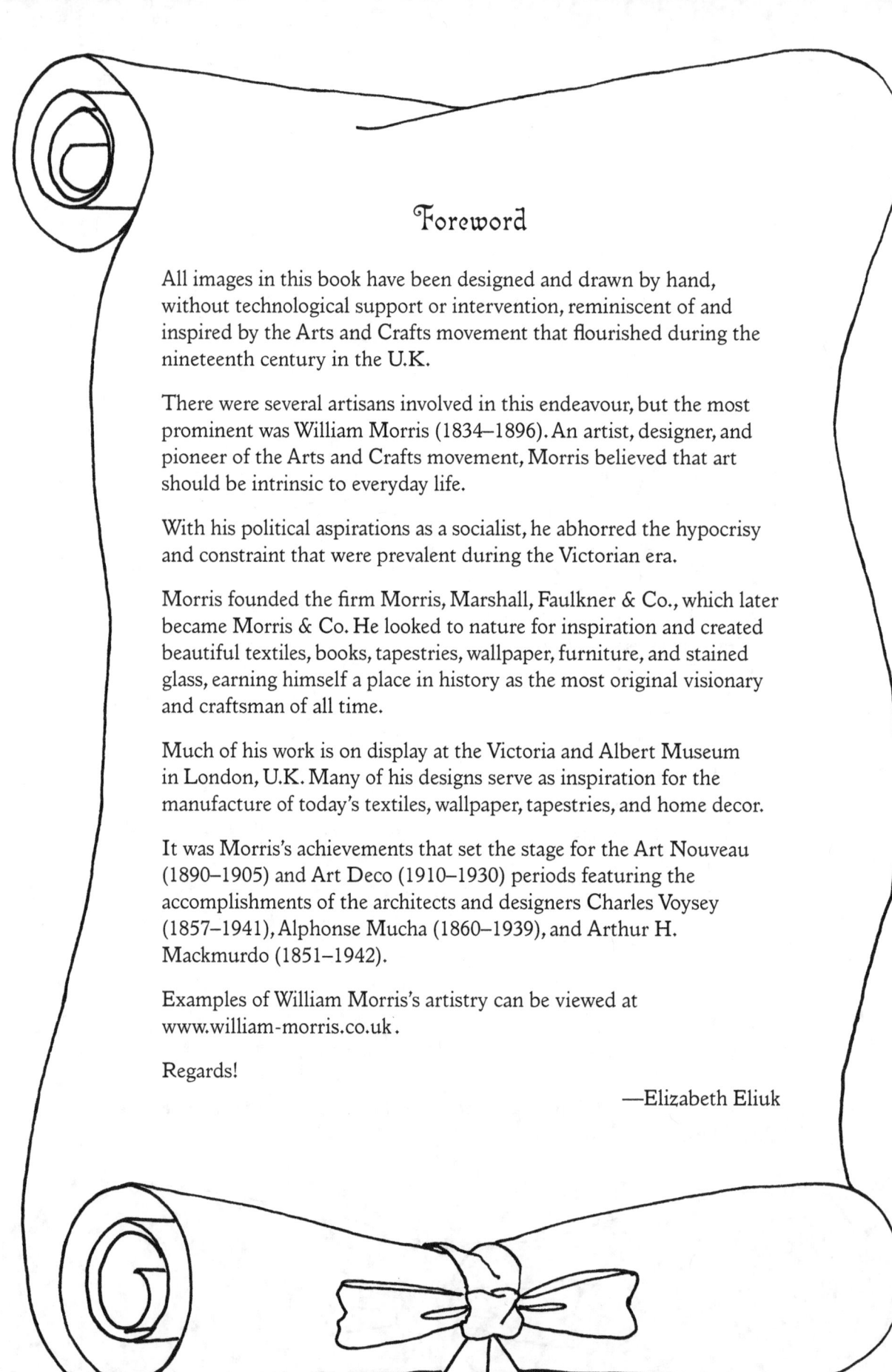

Foreword

All images in this book have been designed and drawn by hand, without technological support or intervention, reminiscent of and inspired by the Arts and Crafts movement that flourished during the nineteenth century in the U.K.

There were several artisans involved in this endeavour, but the most prominent was William Morris (1834–1896). An artist, designer, and pioneer of the Arts and Crafts movement, Morris believed that art should be intrinsic to everyday life.

With his political aspirations as a socialist, he abhorred the hypocrisy and constraint that were prevalent during the Victorian era.

Morris founded the firm Morris, Marshall, Faulkner & Co., which later became Morris & Co. He looked to nature for inspiration and created beautiful textiles, books, tapestries, wallpaper, furniture, and stained glass, earning himself a place in history as the most original visionary and craftsman of all time.

Much of his work is on display at the Victoria and Albert Museum in London, U.K. Many of his designs serve as inspiration for the manufacture of today's textiles, wallpaper, tapestries, and home decor.

It was Morris's achievements that set the stage for the Art Nouveau (1890–1905) and Art Deco (1910–1930) periods featuring the accomplishments of the architects and designers Charles Voysey (1857–1941), Alphonse Mucha (1860–1939), and Arthur H. Mackmurdo (1851–1942).

Examples of William Morris's artistry can be viewed at www.william-morris.co.uk.

Regards!

—Elizabeth Eliuk

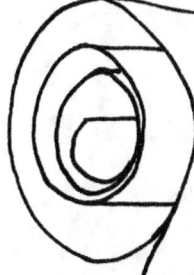

A Mini Art Lesson

There are no rules to colouring except to relax, enjoy yourself, and have fun!

To guide you along the way, I've provided a few hints and instructions with the understanding that you, the colourist, can and should use the information provided as suggestions.

1. If you choose to use coloured pencils, which I recommend, deciding which brand is suitable can be daunting and confusing, considering the variety available in today's market.

    i. **Premier Prisma Coloured Pencils**: these are my favourite and are available in sets of 36, 72, 132, and 150. They are wax-based, providing a creamy-smooth, semi-opaque application. Because of their translucency, each subsequent layer is visible, allowing intermixing of colour in an endless variety. Prismas are the most economical, and like most brands can be easily obtained at your nearest art supply outlet. There is one drawback to wax-based pencils: after applying several layers, there will develop what is referred to as *wax bloom*, giving your work a dull appearance. This can be removed with a soft tissue and gently polishing the applied colour. A fixative designed specifically for coloured pencil can be used not only to seal and protect your work, but to eliminate wax bloom. My favourite brands are Krylon and Grumbacher workable fixative. "Workable" means you can spray a light coating and continue to add more layers of coloured pencil.

    ii. **Faber Castell Polychromos** are available in sets of up to 120 pencils. Unlike the Prismas, these possess an oil base. They also have a tendency to smear easily, and often the colour needs to be reapplied. Avoid this by working left to right (or right to left, depending on which hand you use).

    iii. **Derwent Colorsoft**: available in Student or Professional grades. These come in sets of up to 120. They have a more 'chalky' consistency but layer colours beautifully. They do not possess the Prismas' vibrancy of colour.

    iv. **Caran d'Ache Luminance** provide sets of up to 120. They are oil-based coloured pencils, light-fast and performing the same as the Faber Castell, but they cost considerably more.

All these coloured pencils can be intermixed and used simultaneously.

2. For a pristine clear surface, place a paper towel, tracing paper, or simply another piece of paper under your hand as you work. This will prevent the transfer of oils from your skin to the paper and protect the areas already completed.

3. Use a soft brush (a paintbrush, for example) to sweep away any bits & pieces of pigment that may get deposited, especially after sharpening your pencil.

4. i. Always use your pencils with a sharp point. It is more feasible and economical to use a hand-held sharpener, as electric sharpeners tend to 'eat' your pencil.

   ii. The paper in this book is of an excellent quality and thickness, allowing for multiple layers of pencil. The sharper the point on your pencil, the easier it is to deposit and layer colour.

5. Keep in mind that the colour of the casing, or in the colour charts provided with some brands, may not accurately indicate the colour of each pencil.

6. If you layer more than one colour and are satisfied with the result, be sure to note the names of the colours used and their corresponding numbers, for your future reference.

7. Coloured pencils can be erased but will leave behind a blush of colour staining the paper. Use caution, as too much or too-heavy erasing will damage the texture of the paper. There are several battery-operated erasers available, but I have found the most efficient is manufactured by Staedtler. A *kneaded eraser* is handy for lifting colour to highlight an area, achieving a more three-dimensional effect.

8. Darken your colours by combining indigo rather than black or grey. This will give your work a 'freshness' and brilliance. The only exception is over yellow, as using a dark blue (indigo) with yellow will give you green. In this instance, use a neutral grey or its complement (see "The Colour Wheel").

9. Gel pens or markers can be used alone or in conjunction with coloured pencils. A word of caution: before applying any type of marker, place a sheet or two of paper underneath the page you are working on to prevent the colour from bleeding onto the next page. Whether you are using coloured pencils or gel pens, it would be to your benefit to insert a couple of untextured sheets of paper in between the pages, to avoid the possibility of the printer's ink being transferred to the underside of the

page. The heavier the pressure applied by your pencil or pen, the greater the chances this may occur. There are several brands of gel pens and markers available. Experimentation and experience is not only enjoyable but the best teacher. Always wait for the gel pen or marker to dry before turning the page or closing the book.

10. Water-based products are not recommended, as they will cause the paper to buckle regardless of the thickness. Even specifically designed watercolour paper requires special preparation to avoid buckling from the use of water-based media.

11. Display your work in your home, or present your creation as a gift to someone special. Never display your work in direct sunlight.

Using This Book

I hope you will find as much pleasure in this book as I have found in creating it.

The images in this book have all been designed keeping you, the colourist, in mind. Whether you are a novice or expert, or somewhere in between, I guarantee your satisfaction whatever your level of expertise.

There is a border around each design for more attractive framing. A "Designation" name page allows you to personalize this book by entering your name and the dates you started & finished. Pages titled "Notes / Reminders to Myself" are provided for your convenience at the back of this book.

If you enjoyed the book, I invite you to post your comments and examples of your artistry on my blog, dashingdiva.blog, or e-mail me at eliuk.elizabeth@gmail.com.

I look forward to hearing from you.

—E.E.

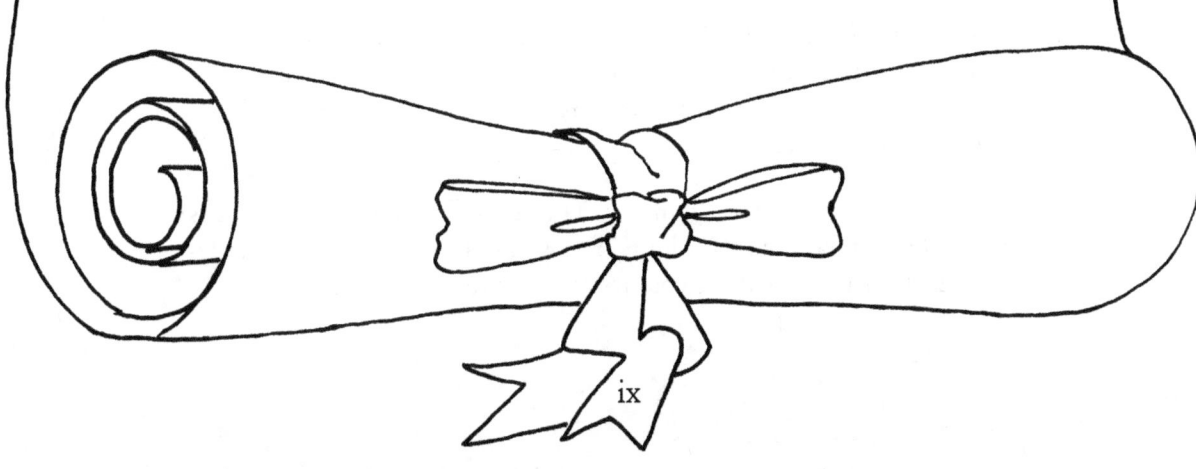

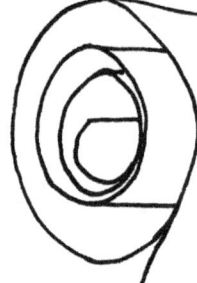

The Colour Wheel

Colour surrounds us everywhere, and how each of us sees and interprets colour is as unique as a fingerprint. Artists develop and utilize a 'personal palette' that they use consistently in all their work.

Colour is defined by three characteristics:

i.   *hue* – the name of the colour,

ii. *value* – the lightness or darkness of the colour, and

iii. *intensity* – defined by the purity or strength of a colour: vivid or dull. "Dull" is not used pejoratively, only to describe it as being opposite of vivid.

The colour wheel will help you understand the basic concepts of colour and determine your own 'palette'.

Primary colours are the three basic colours from which all other colours are mixed, namely red, blue, and yellow.

Secondary colours are obtained by mixing two primary colours, for example orange or green.

Tertiary colours are obtained by mixing a primary and a secondary colour, for example yellow-orange or blue-purple.

Complementary colours are pairs that are positioned directly across the wheel from one another, for example red and green. Mixing the complementaries from your colour wheel will give you a grey.

Analogous colours are close together on the wheel and nearly alike, but slightly different in hue, for example yellow, yellow-green, and green.

Black and white are not considered colours because they have no range of values. White is never lighter or darker as black is neither darker nor lighter. White is to put it simply "white" and the same holds true for black.

But when you mix the black and white, you will get grey and depending on the proportions of each you will now achieve values. Therefore when you add white you create a *tint*, adding grey makes a *tone*, and black a *shade*.

The colour wheel is divided in half. The left side has the *warm* colours; the right side has the *cool* colours. Yellow and purple are on both sides of the wheel, because these colours can be either warm or cool.

A colour wheel has been purposely left blank of all colour, but providing the names of the hues in each category. It is left for you to choose your own colours and fill in the blanks, giving attention to the specified sections. Layer your primaries to give you the secondary / analogous / tertiary combinations as indicated in the legend below the colour wheel.

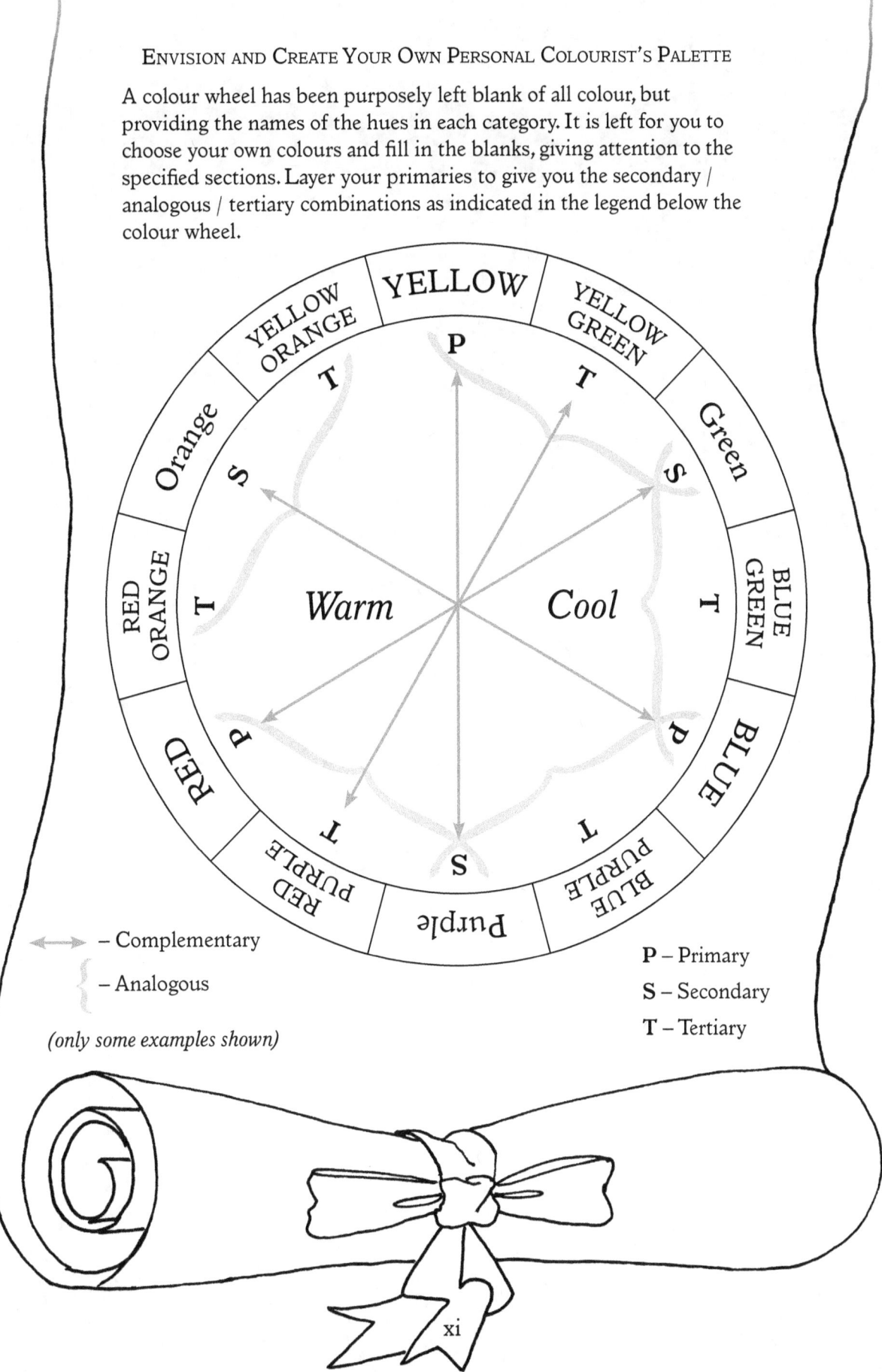

— Complementary

— Analogous

(only some examples shown)

P – Primary

S – Secondary

T – Tertiary

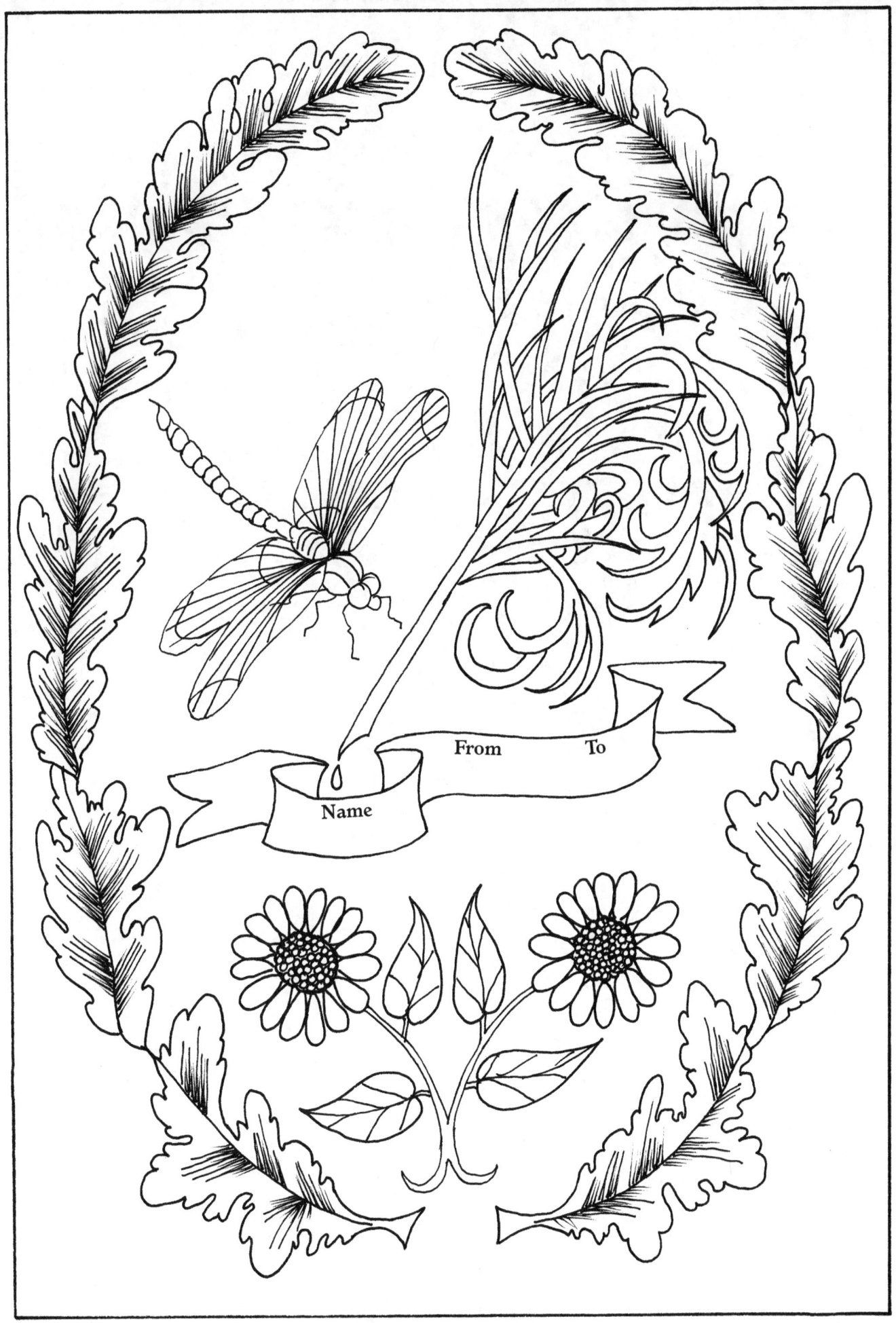

Name   From   To

DESIGNATION PAGE

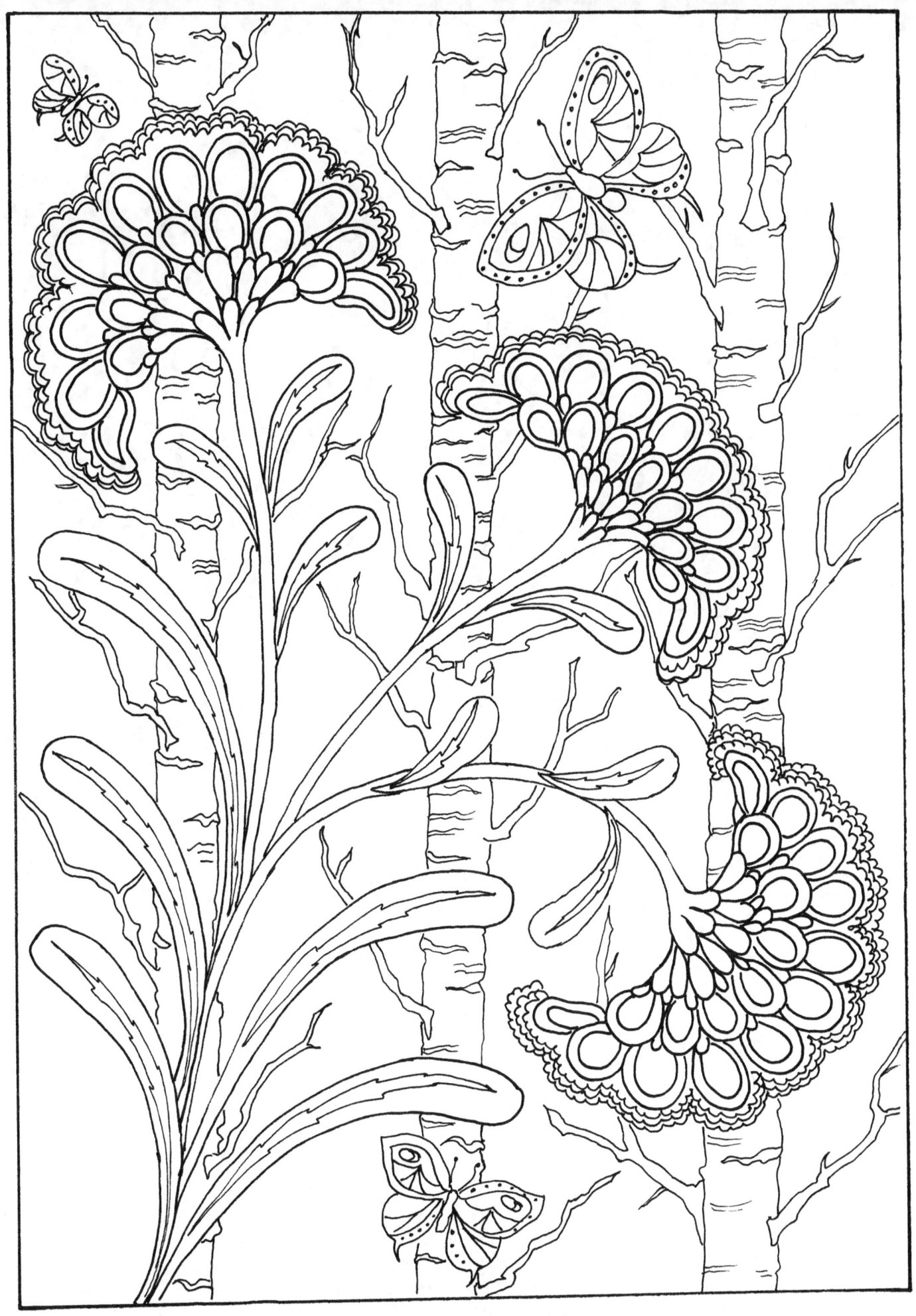

1. ZINNIAS AND BIRCH TREES

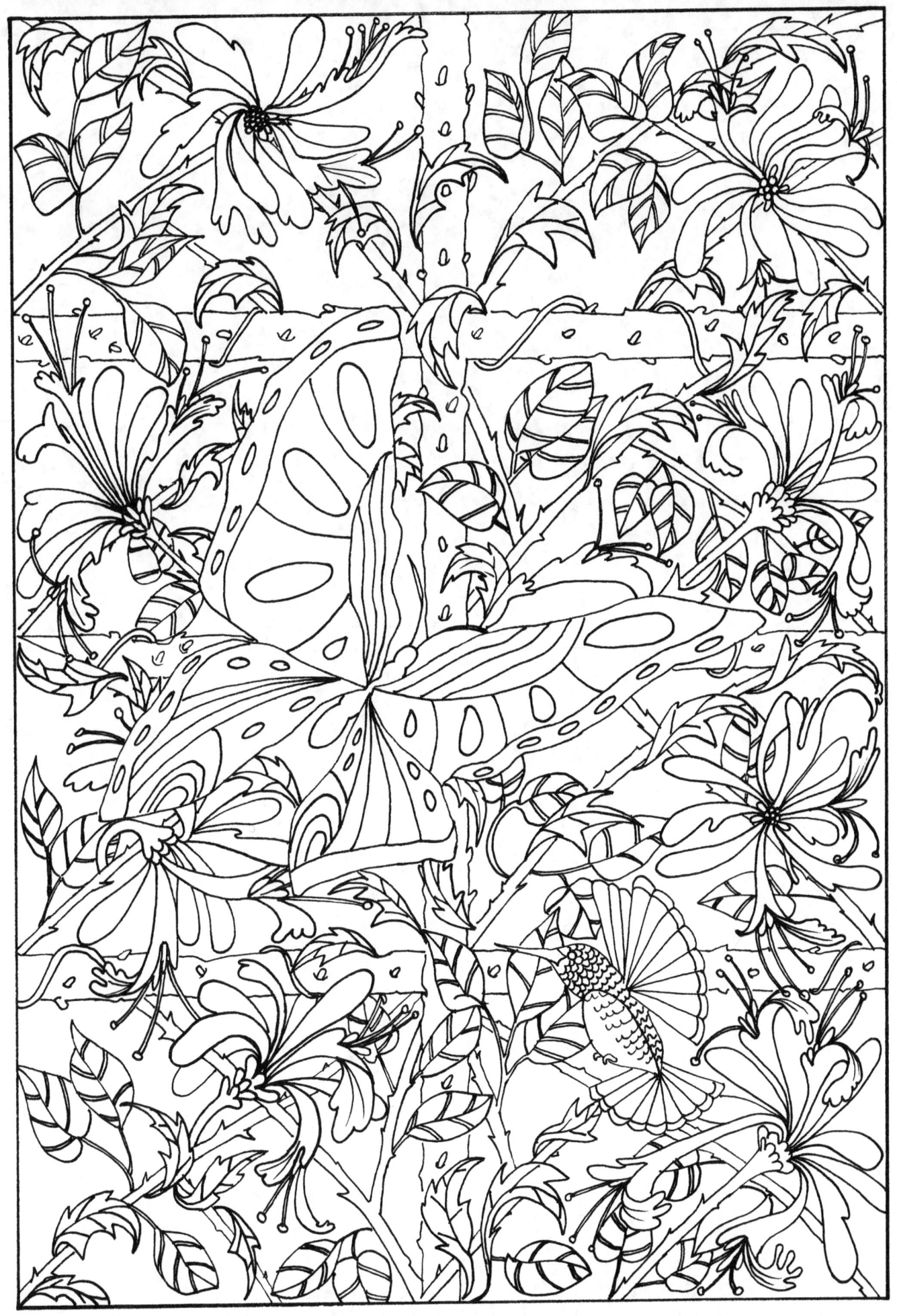

2. Honeysuckle Vine Trellis

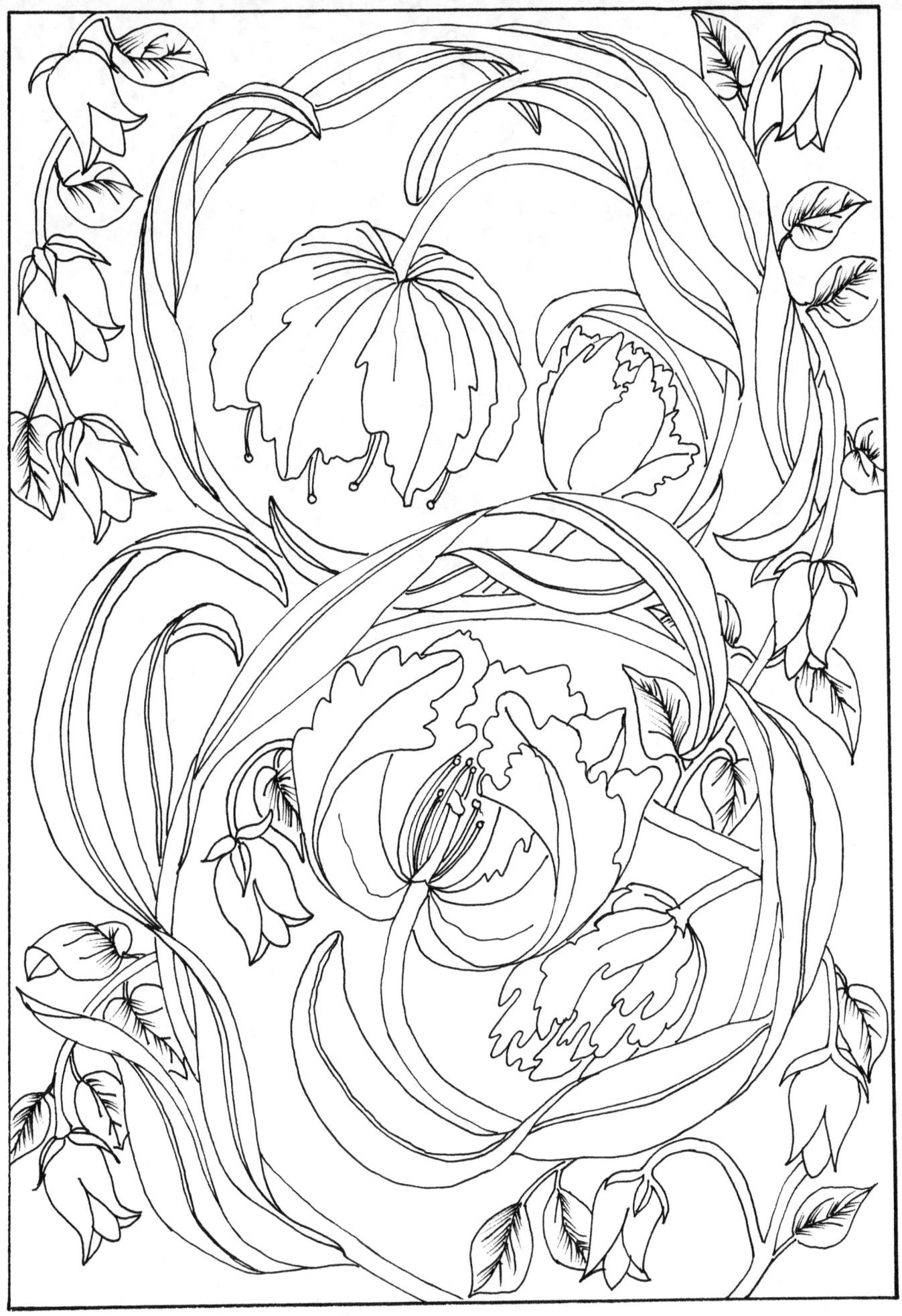

3. TULIPS AND BLUEBELLS

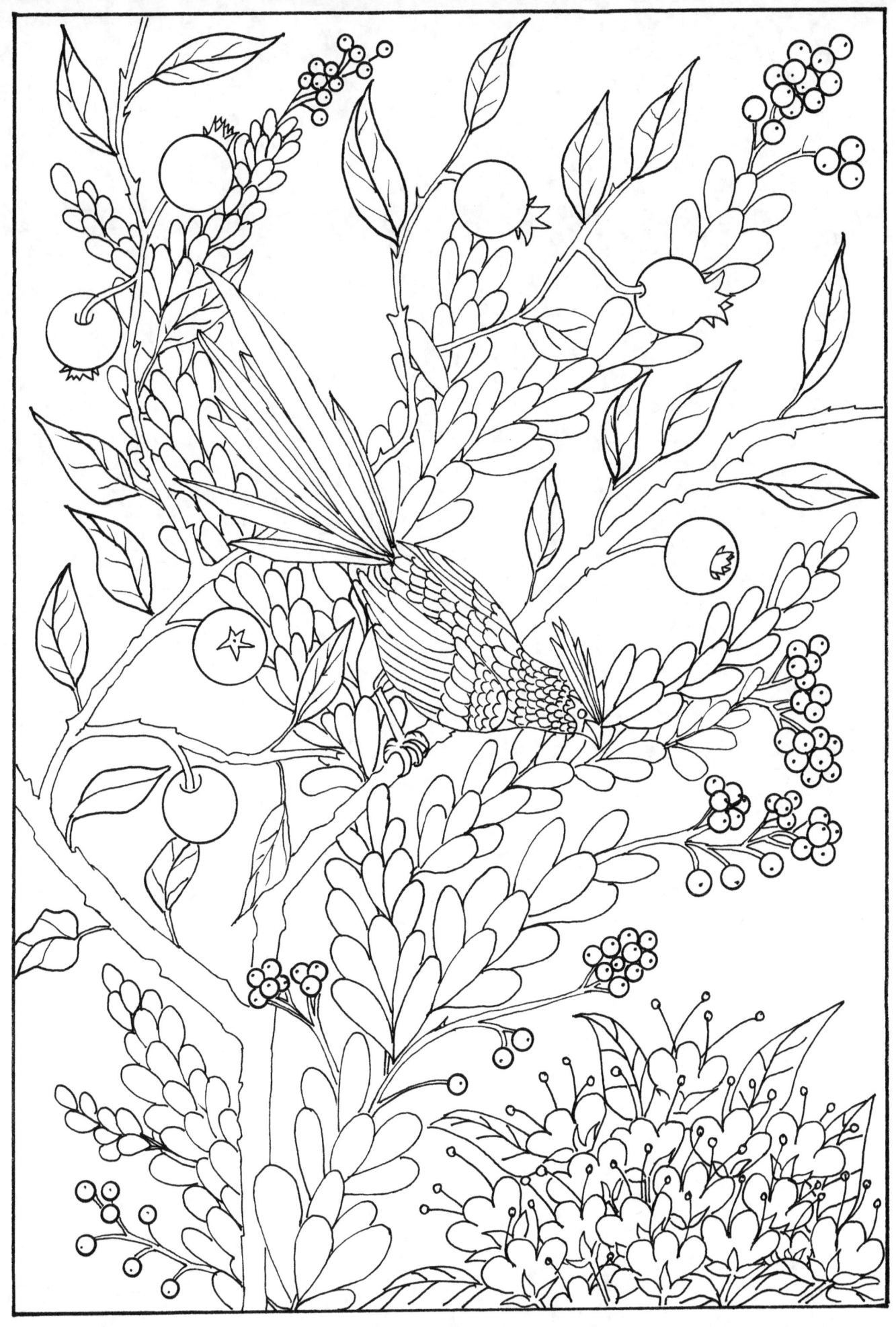

4. BIRD, CRABAPPLES, AND BOXWOOD

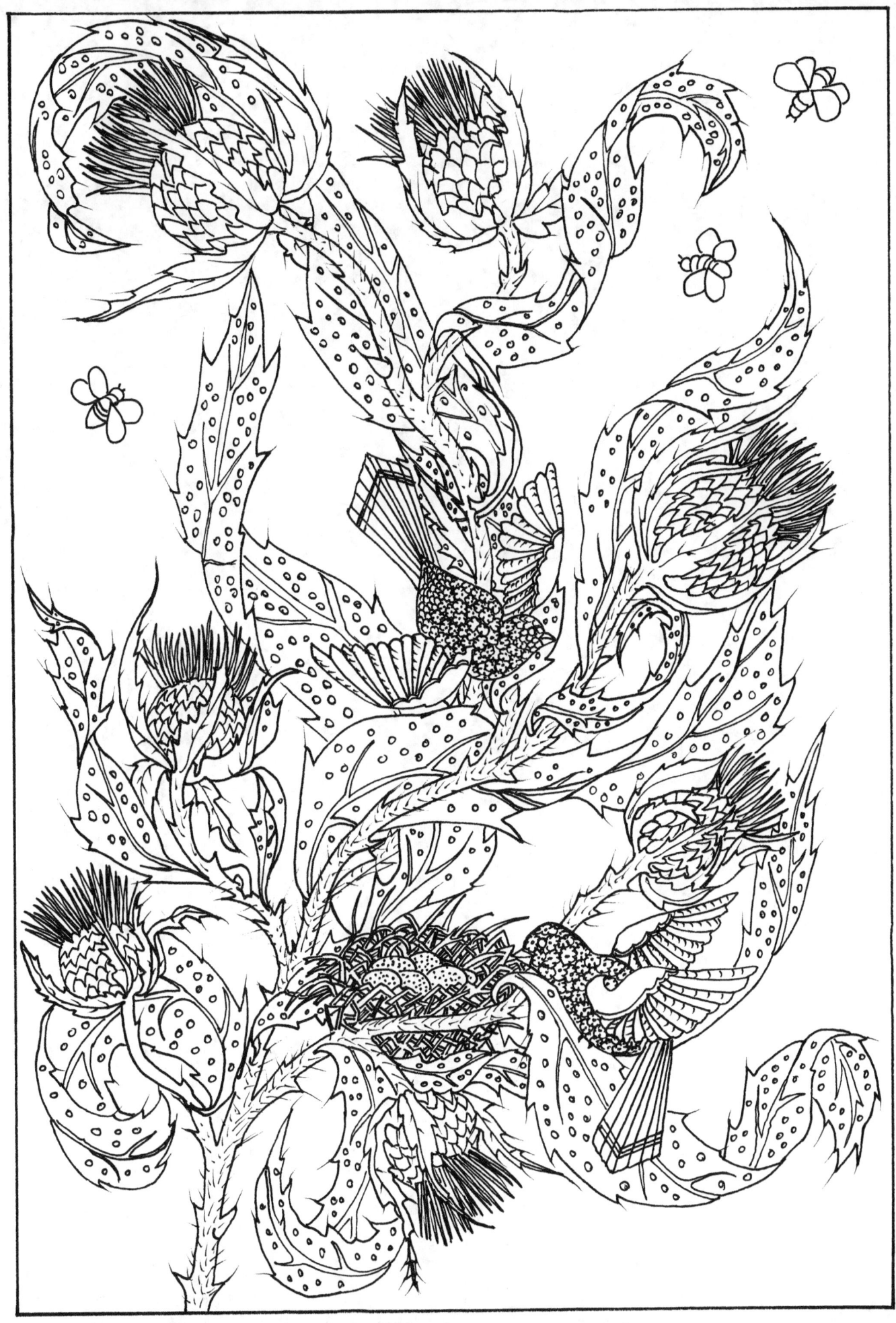

5. BULL THISTLE AND FINCHES

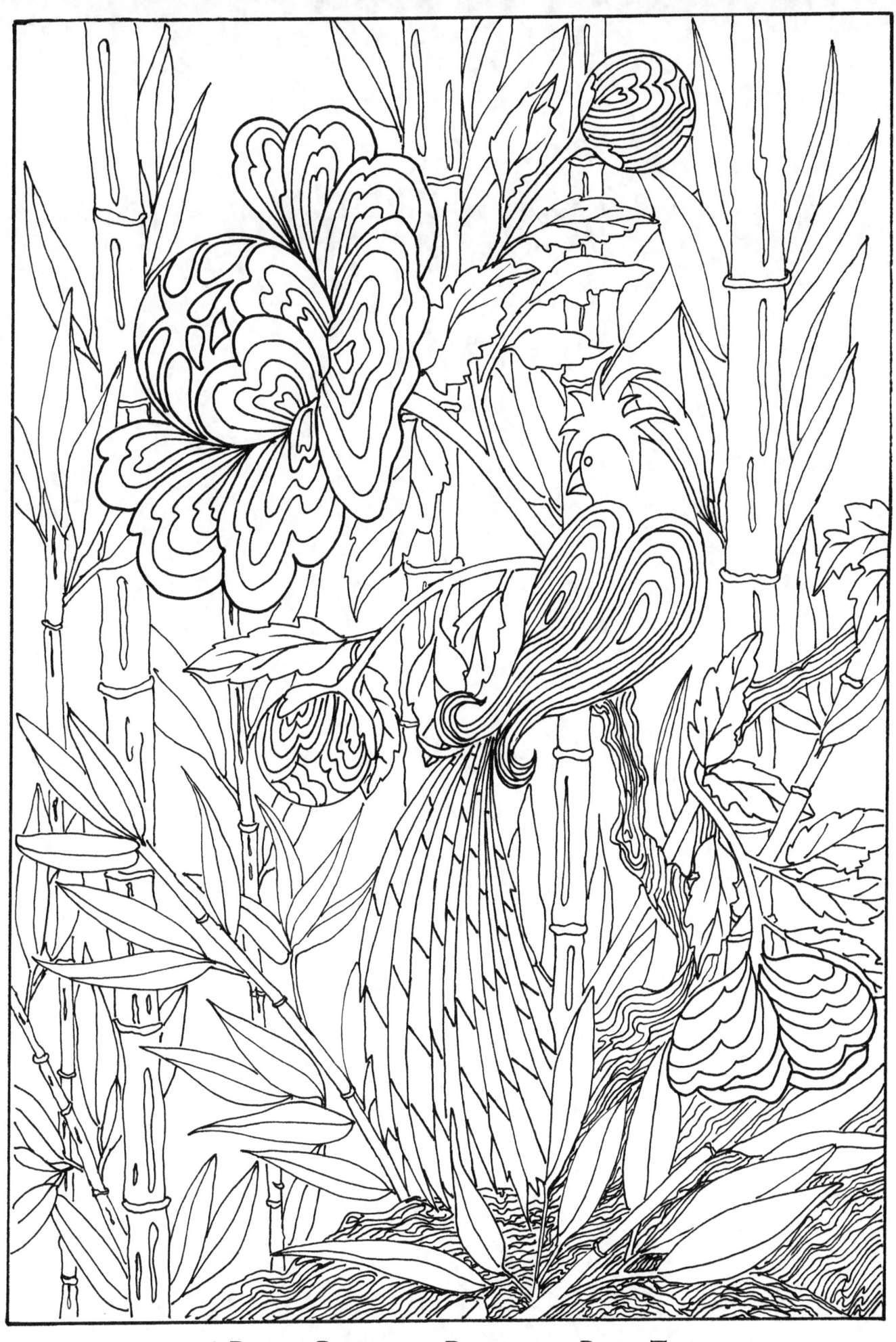

6 BIRD OF PARADISE IN BAMBOO AND PEONY TREE

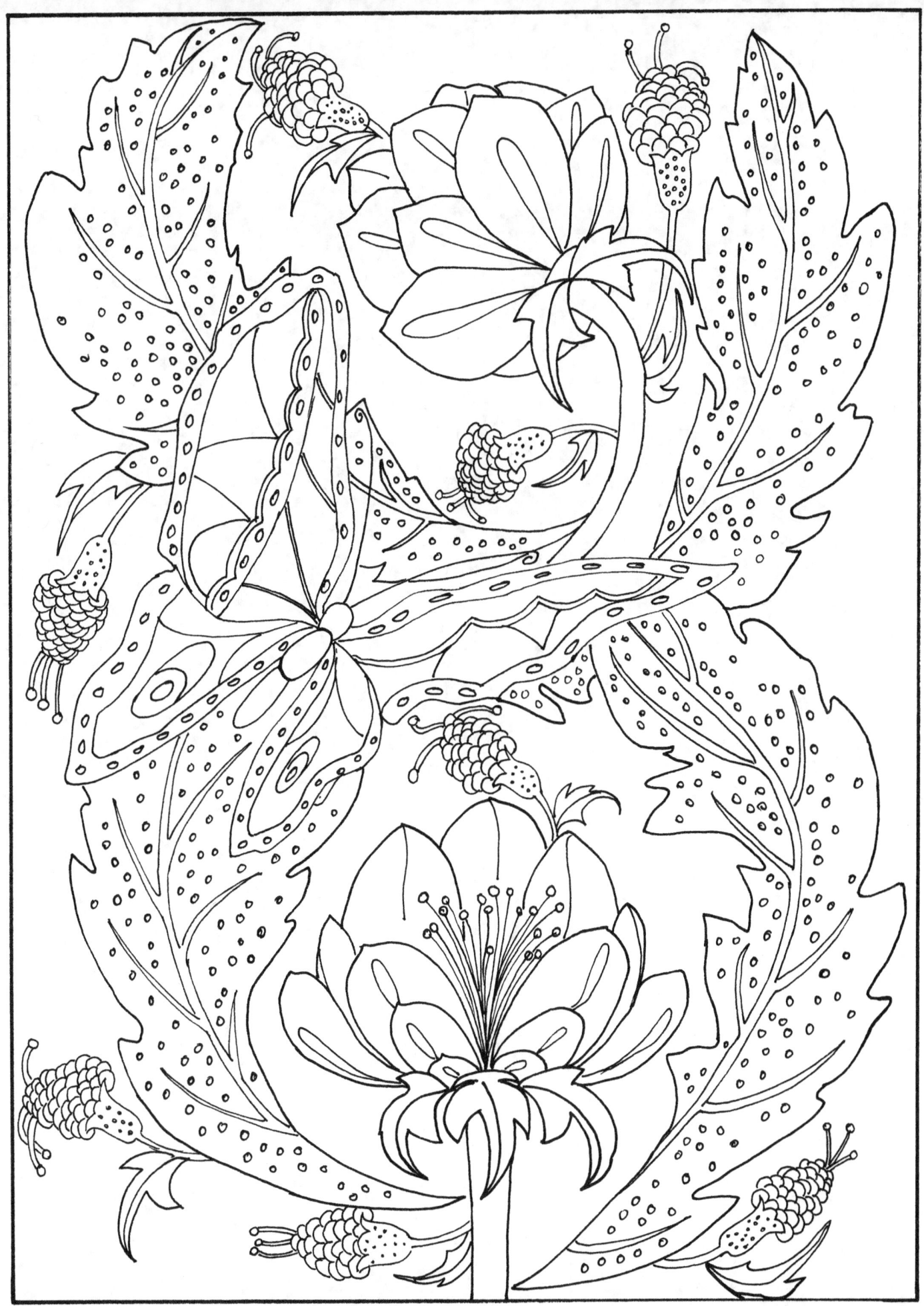

7. ANEMONES AND BUTTERFLY

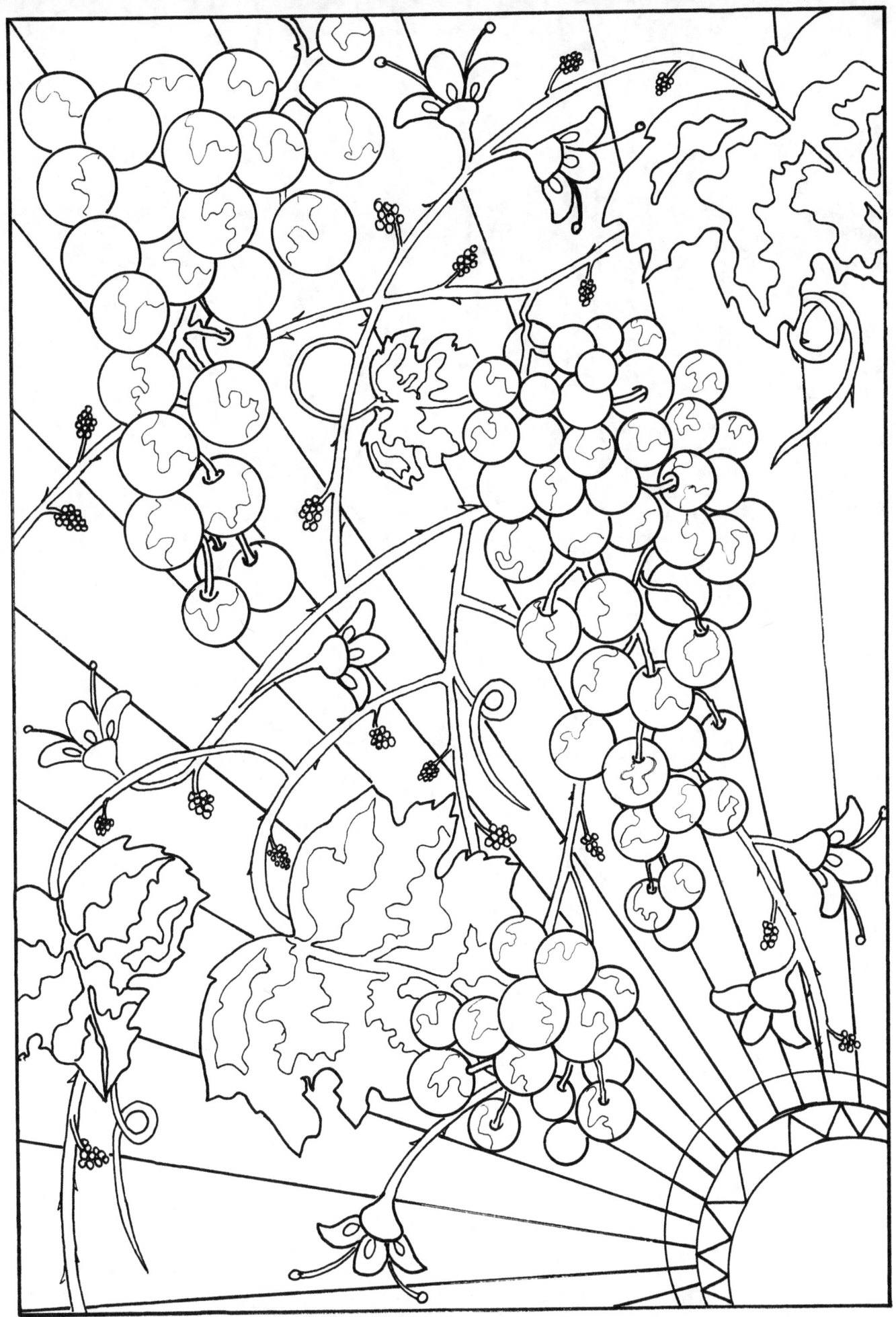

8. SUN-RIPENED GRAPES

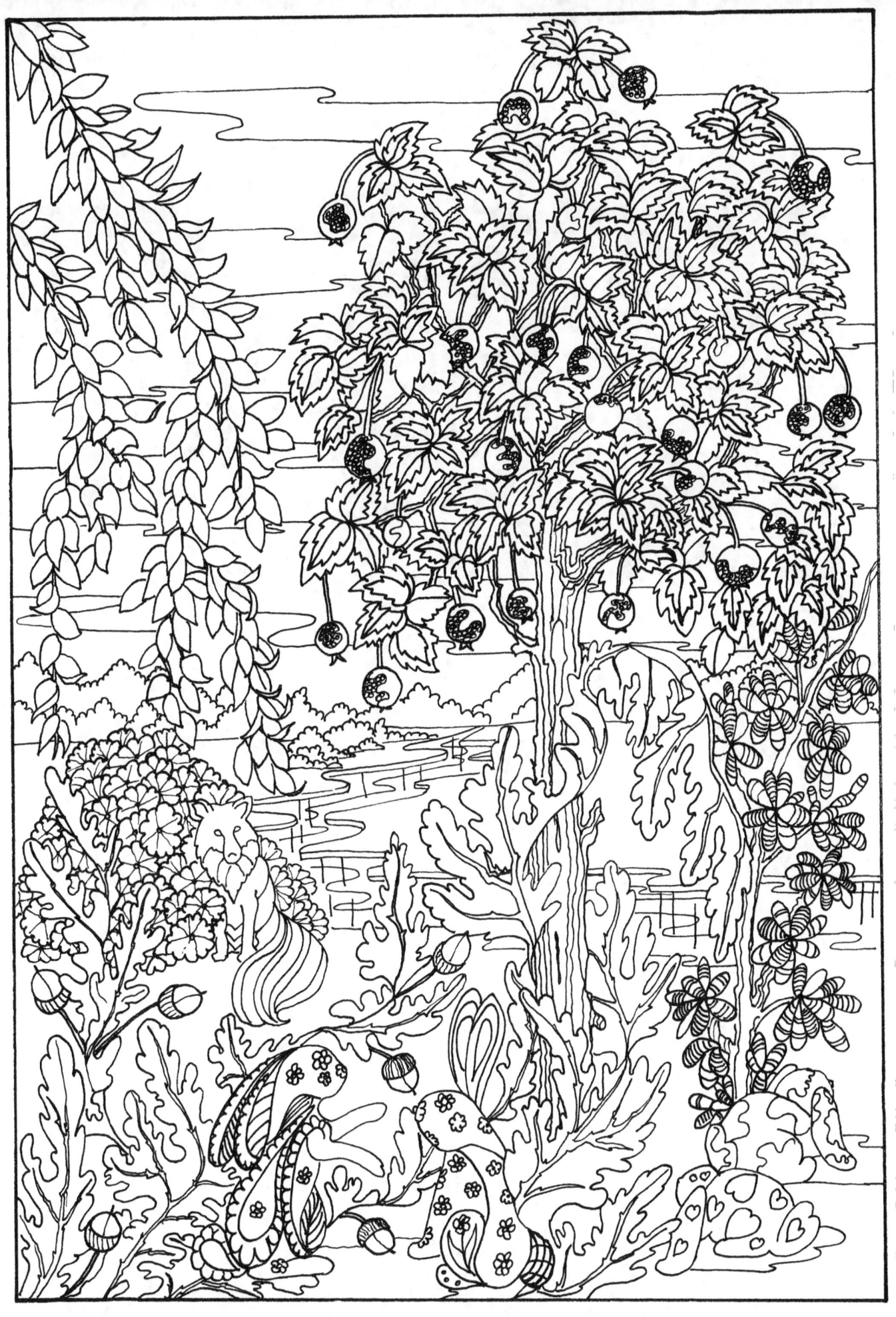

9. Playful Hares under Pomegranate Trees

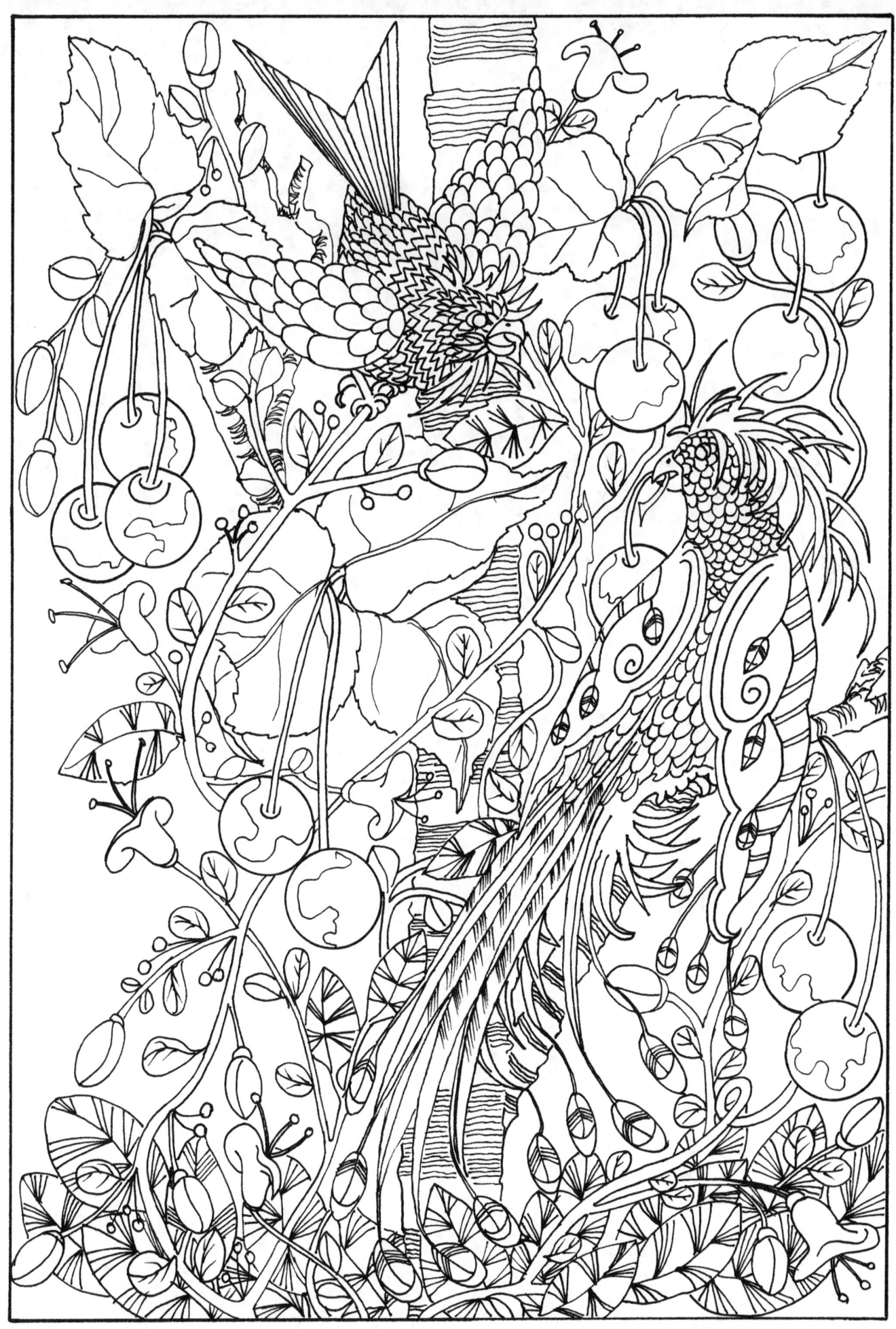

10. CHERRY PICKER RIVALS

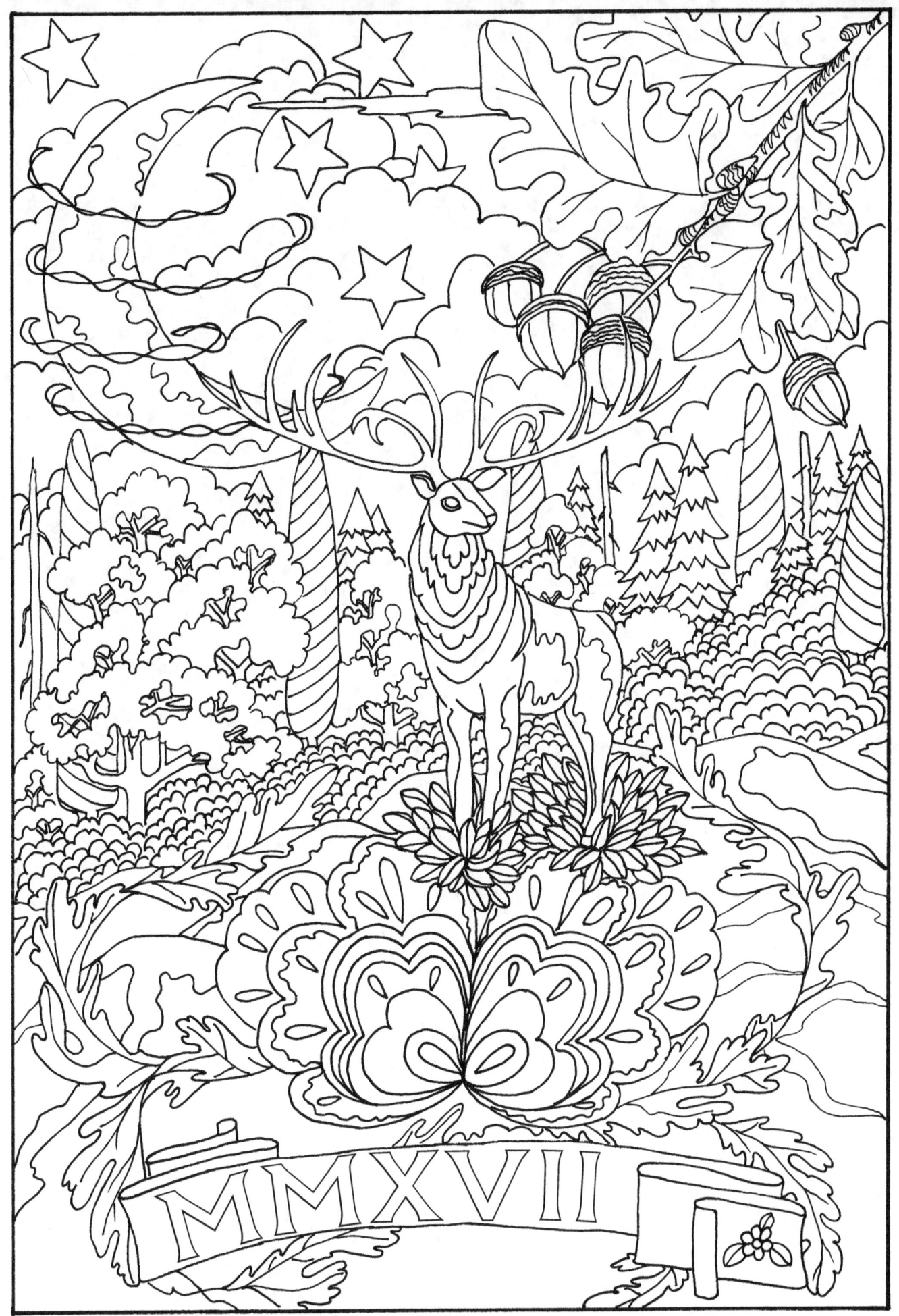

11. ROYAL STAG

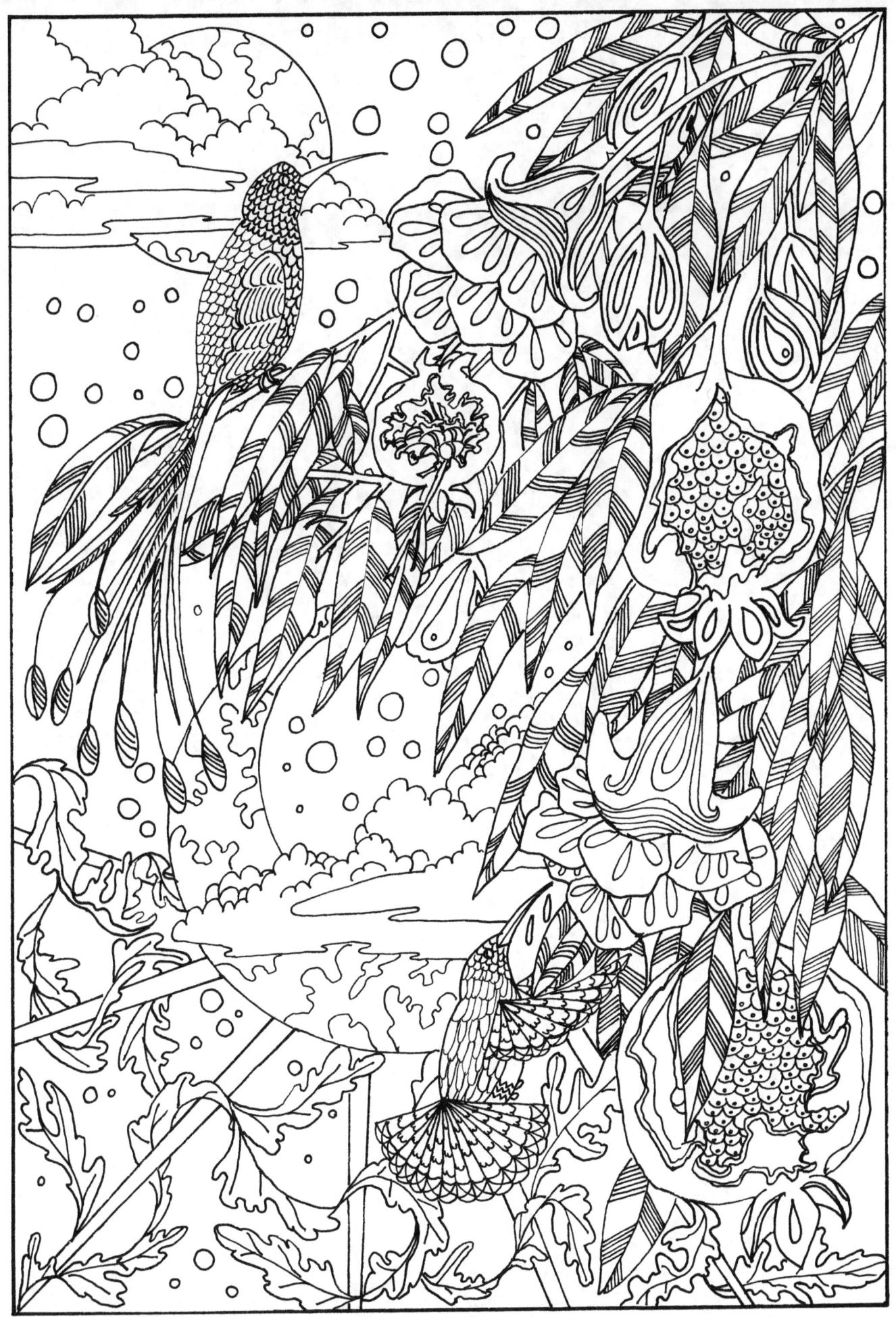

12. Pomegranate Dwellers

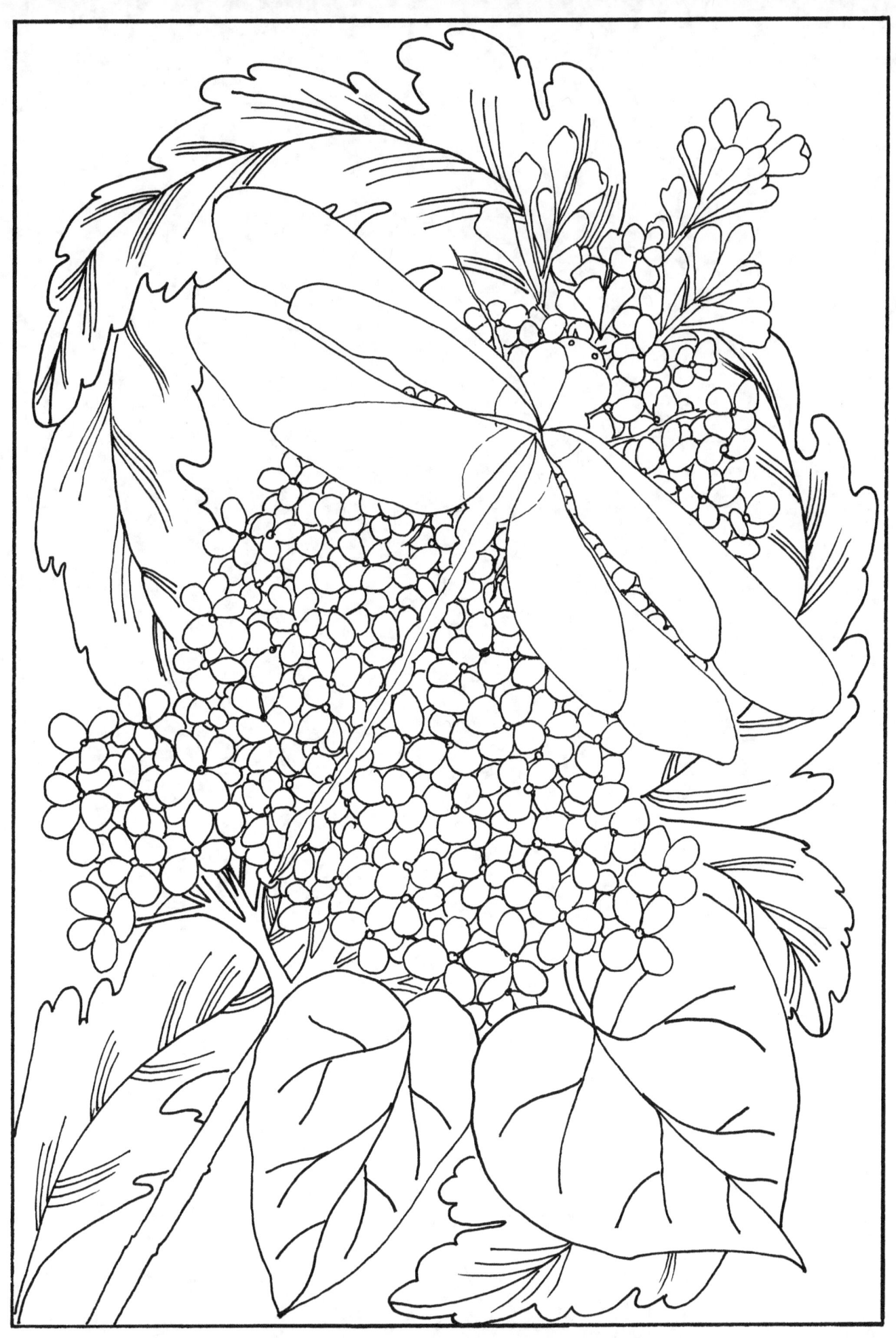

13. VISITING DRAGONFLY – *design your own wings*

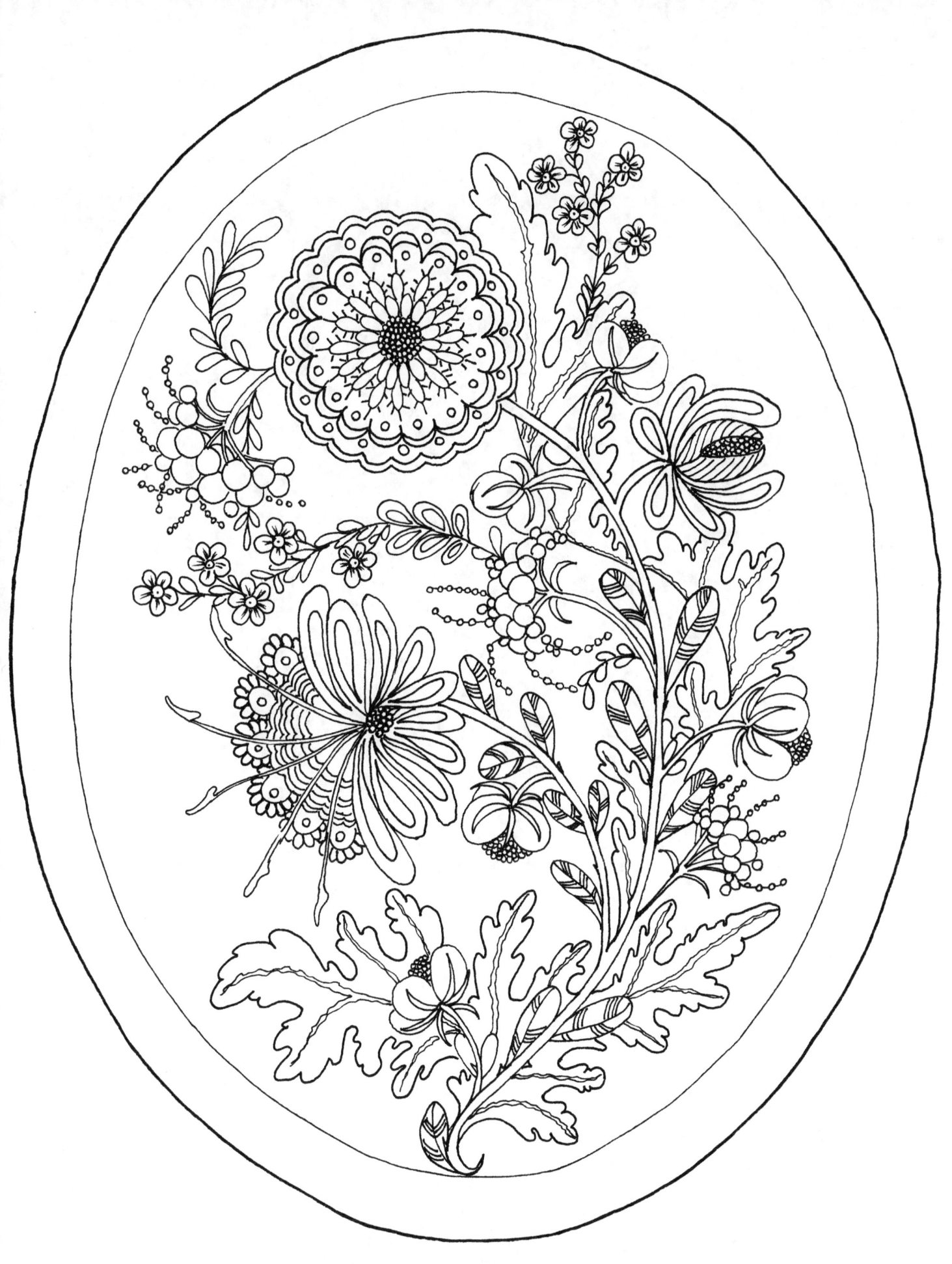

14. OVAL BLOOMS – *design your own border*

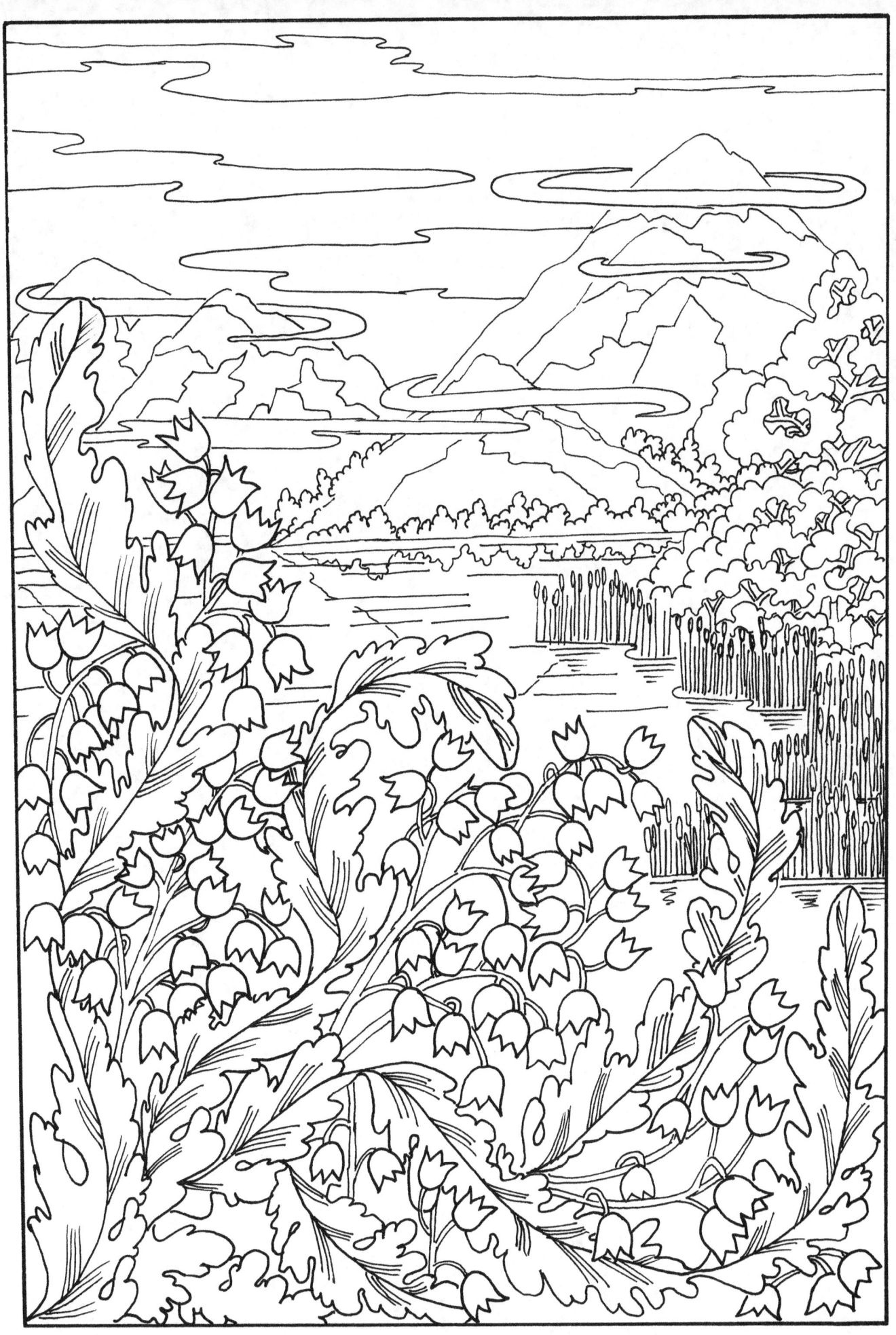

15. Lily of the Valley

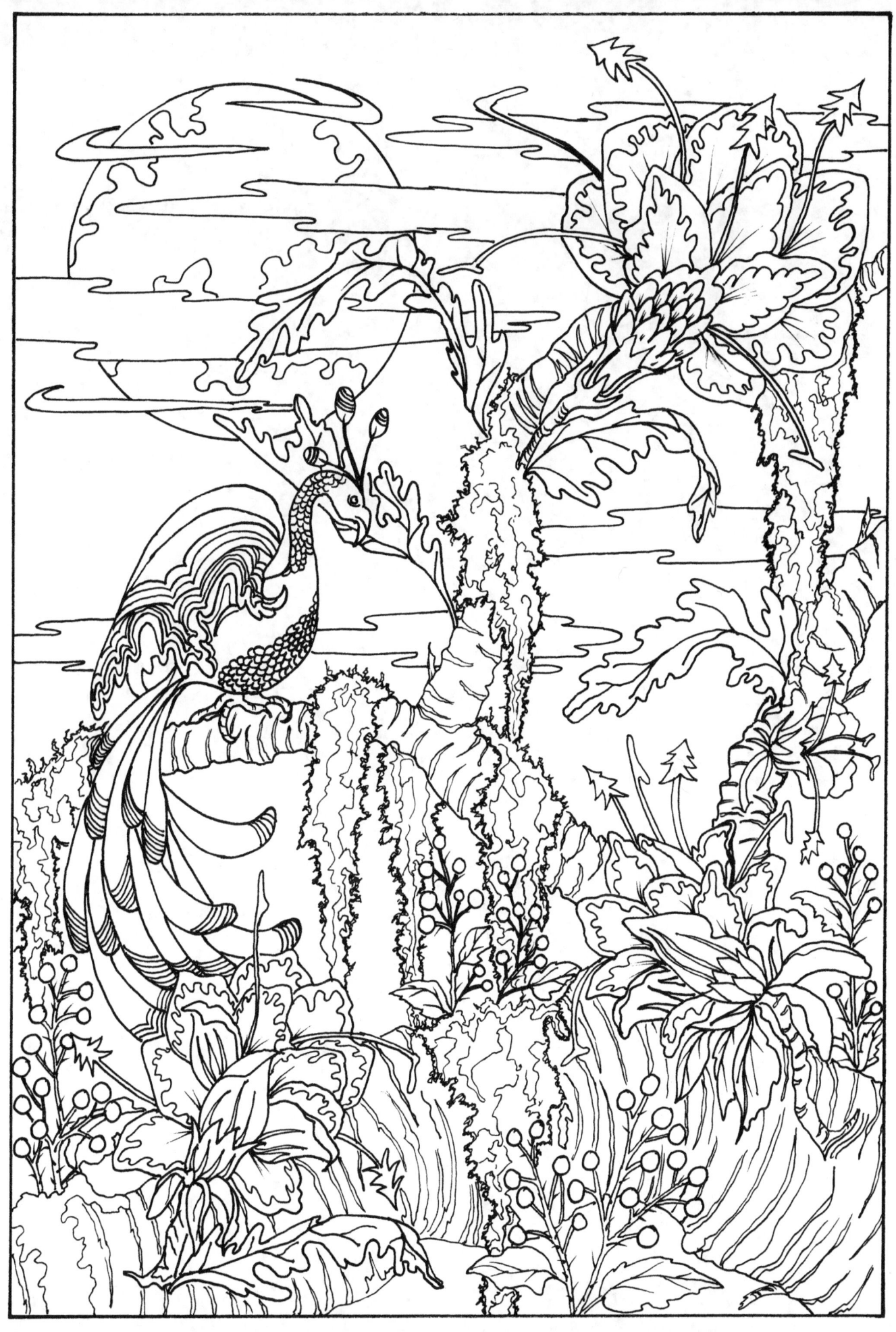

16. Exotic Bird in Tree with Moss and Flowers

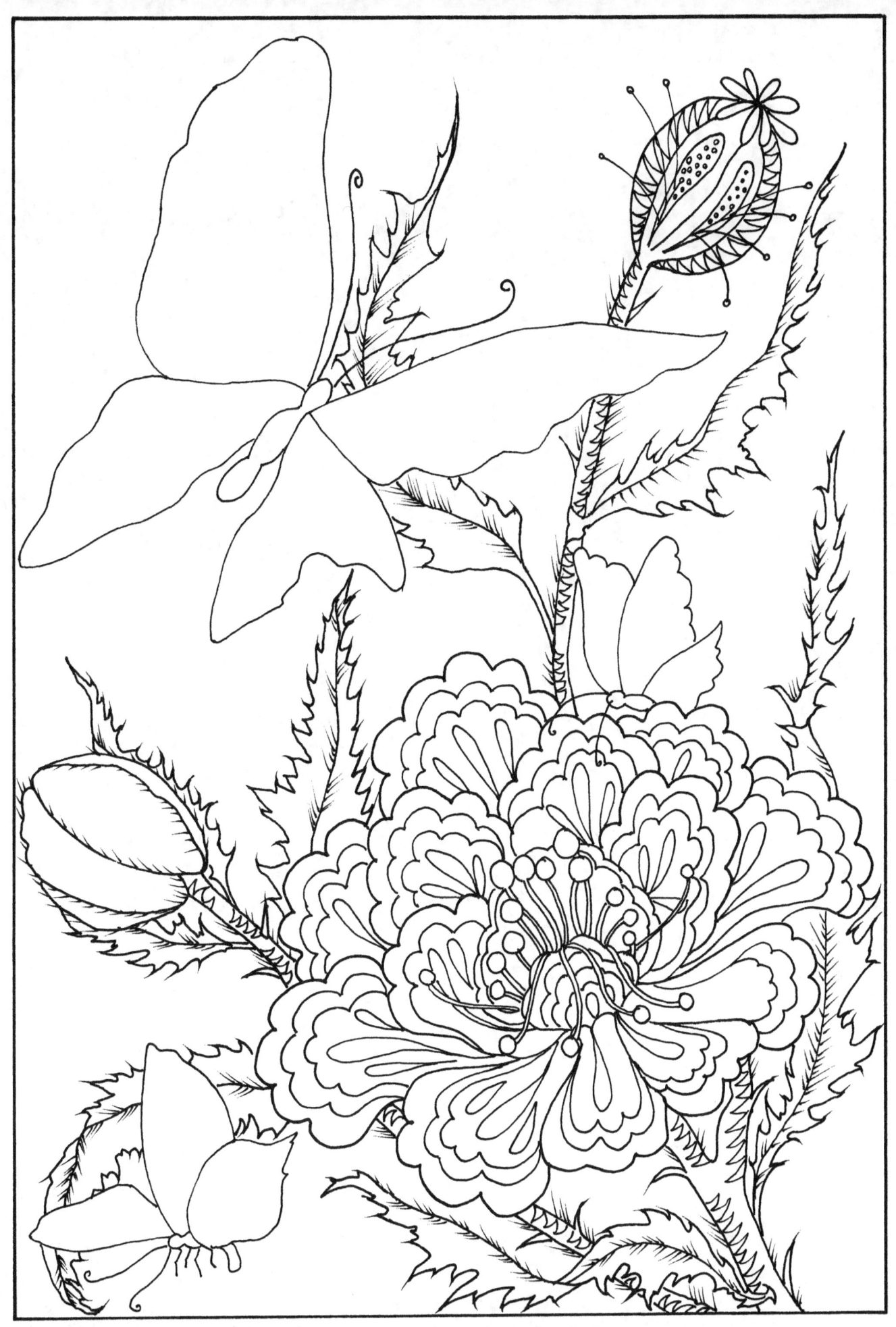

17. POPPY – *design your own butterflies*

18. Turtle Doves

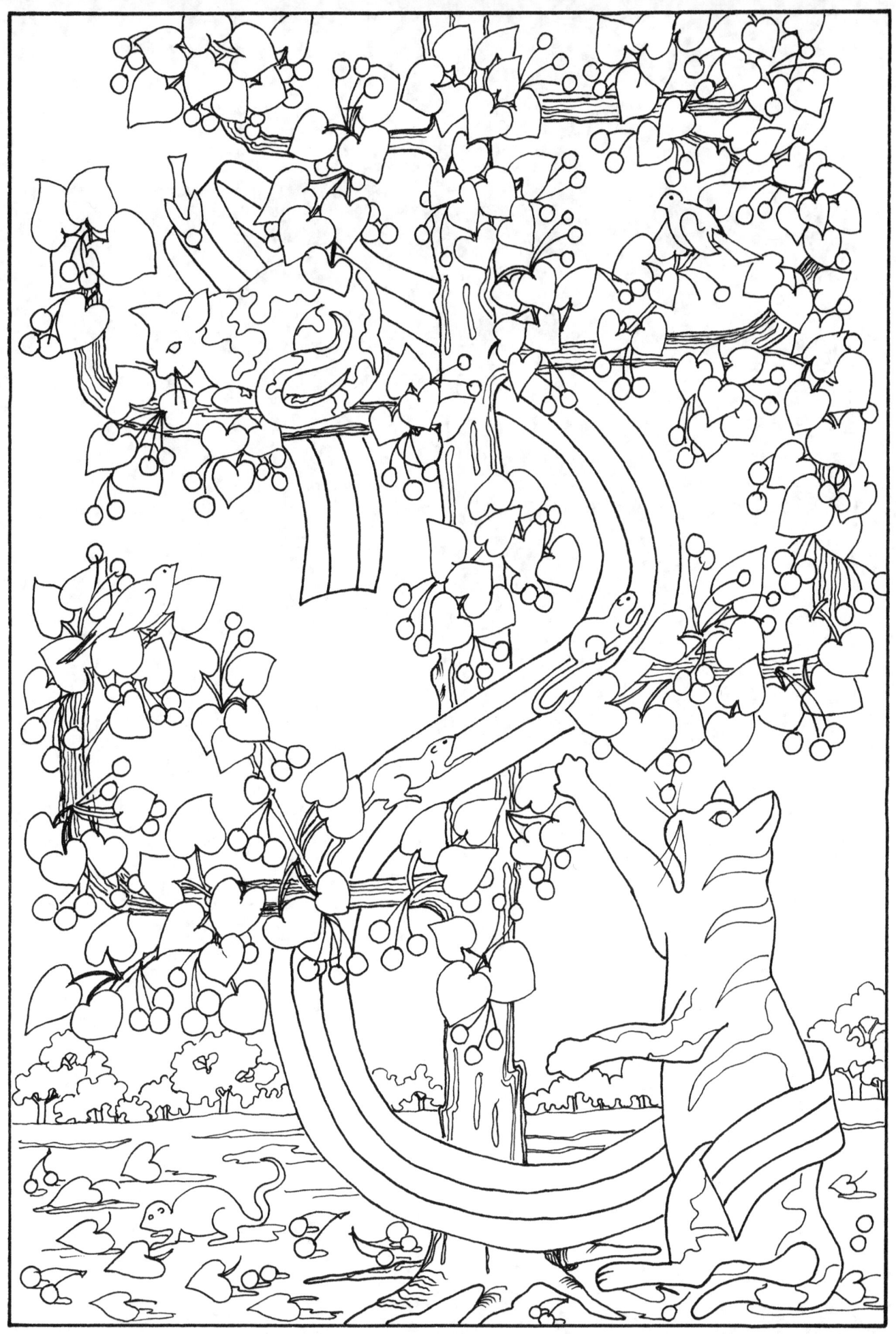

19. A Cat's Temptations

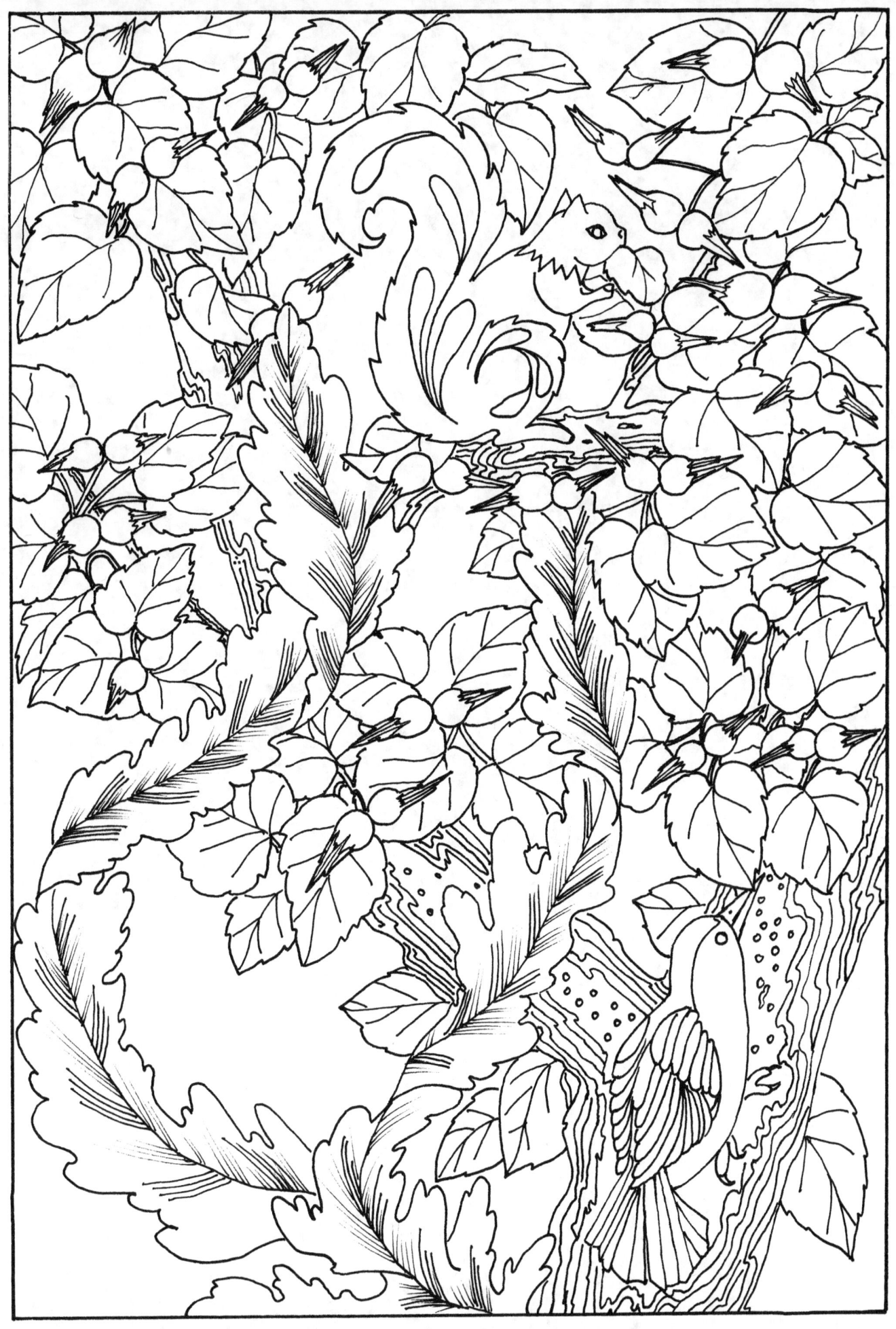

20. WOODPECKER WITH SQUIRREL

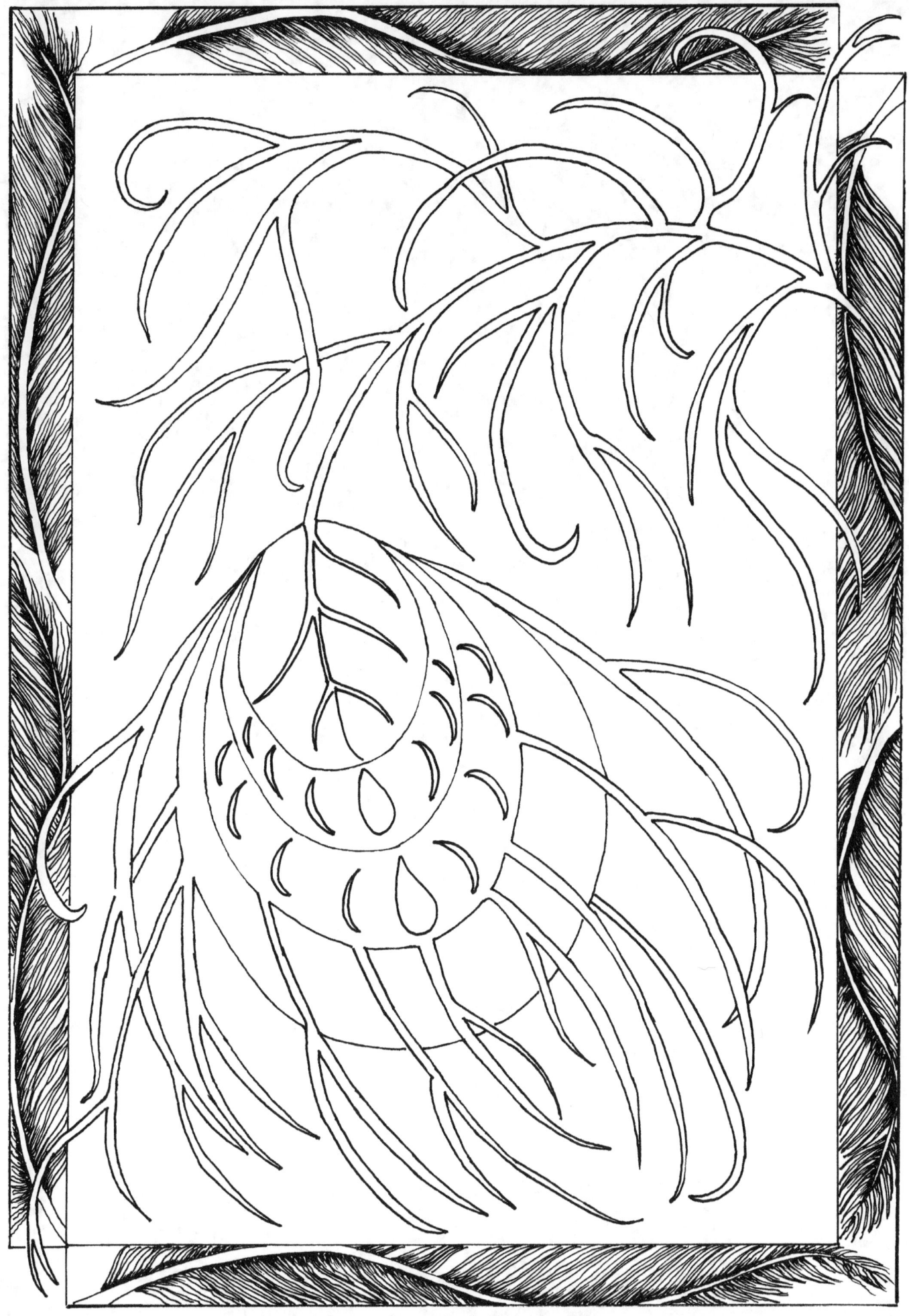

21. PEACOCK FEATHER

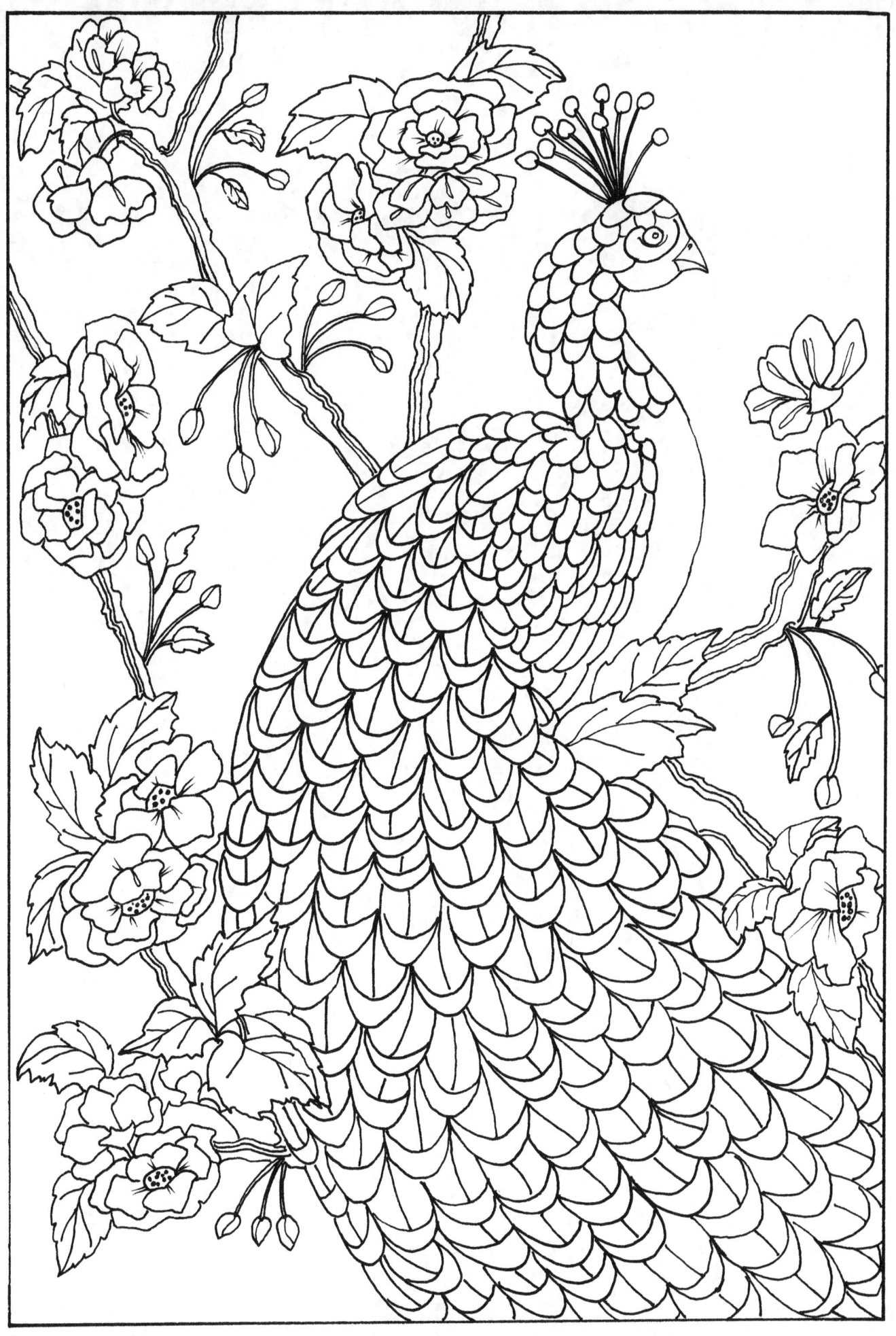

22. Peacock with Camellia Blossoms

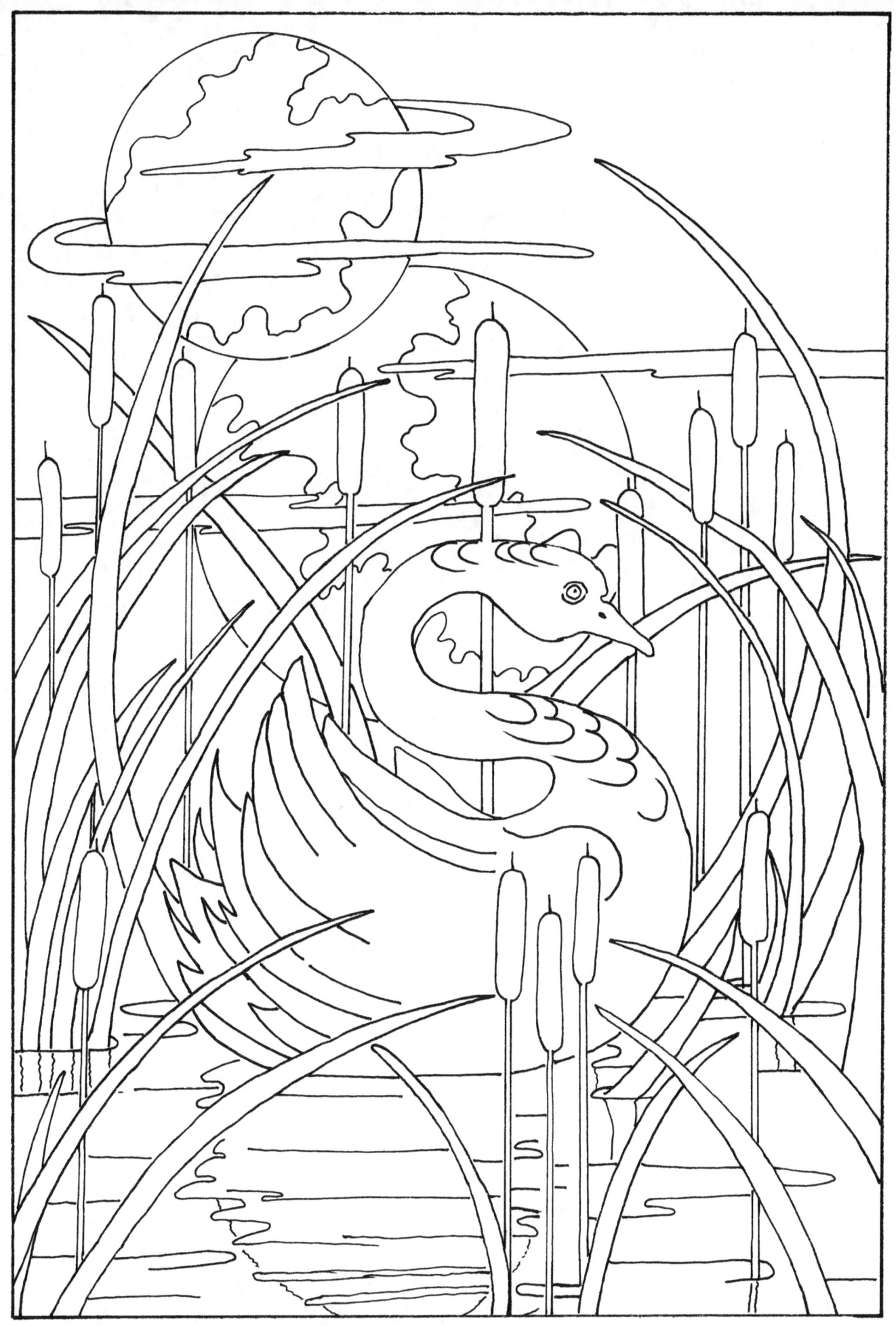

23. Swan and Cattails

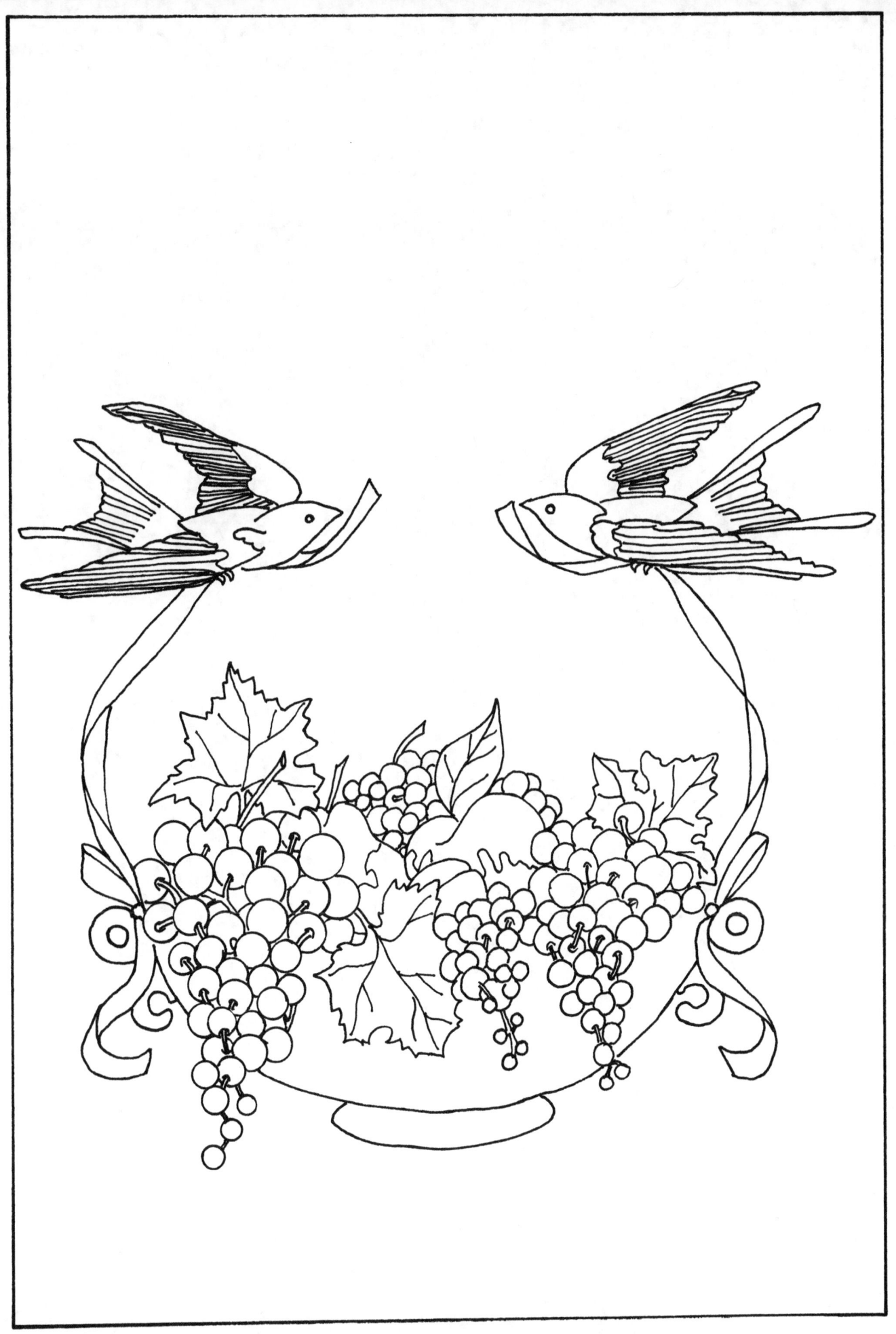

24. FRUIT BEARERS – *design your own background*

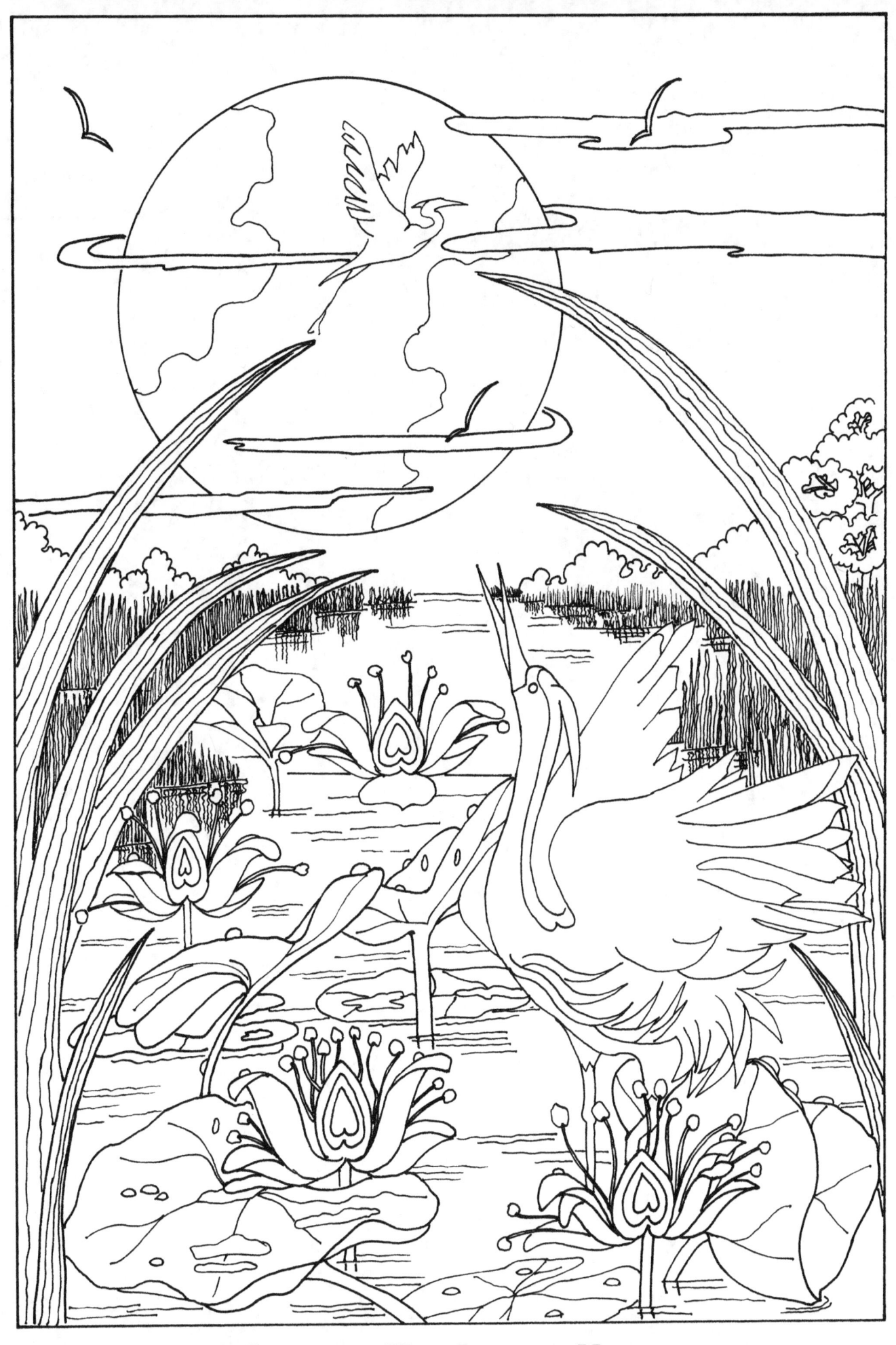

25. CRANES WITH WATER LILIES AND MOONLIGHT

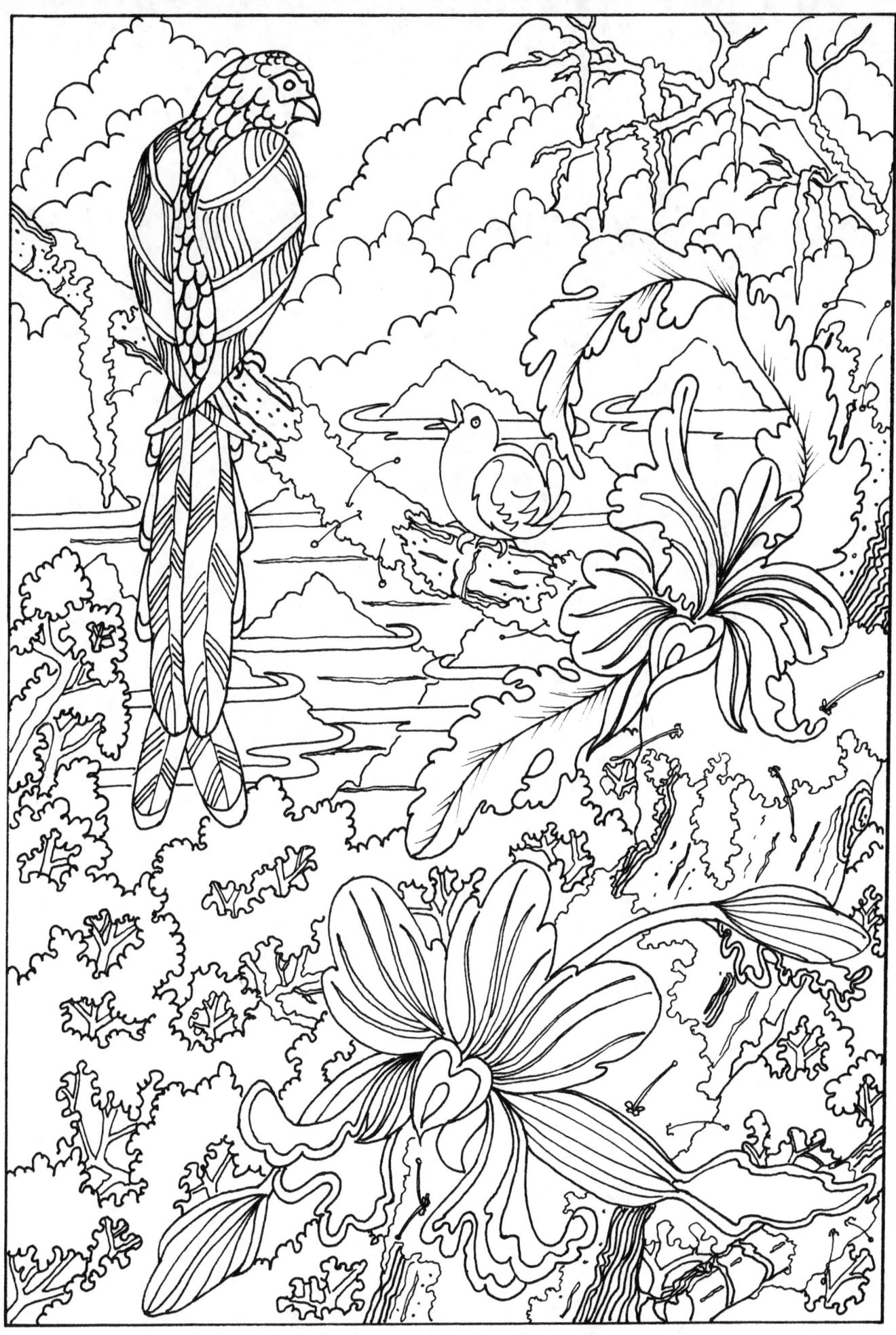

26. ORCHIDS WITH BIRDS IN TREE

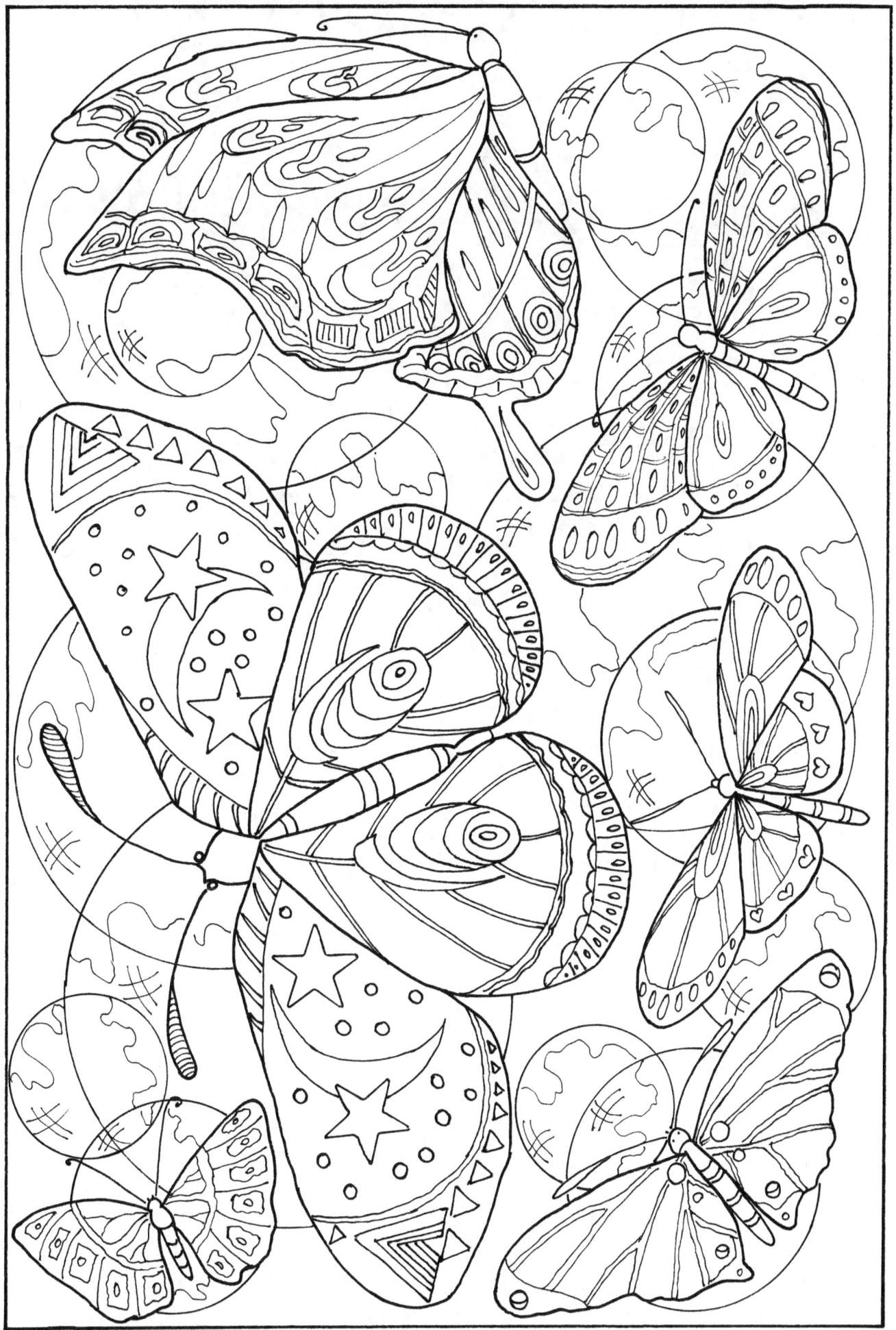

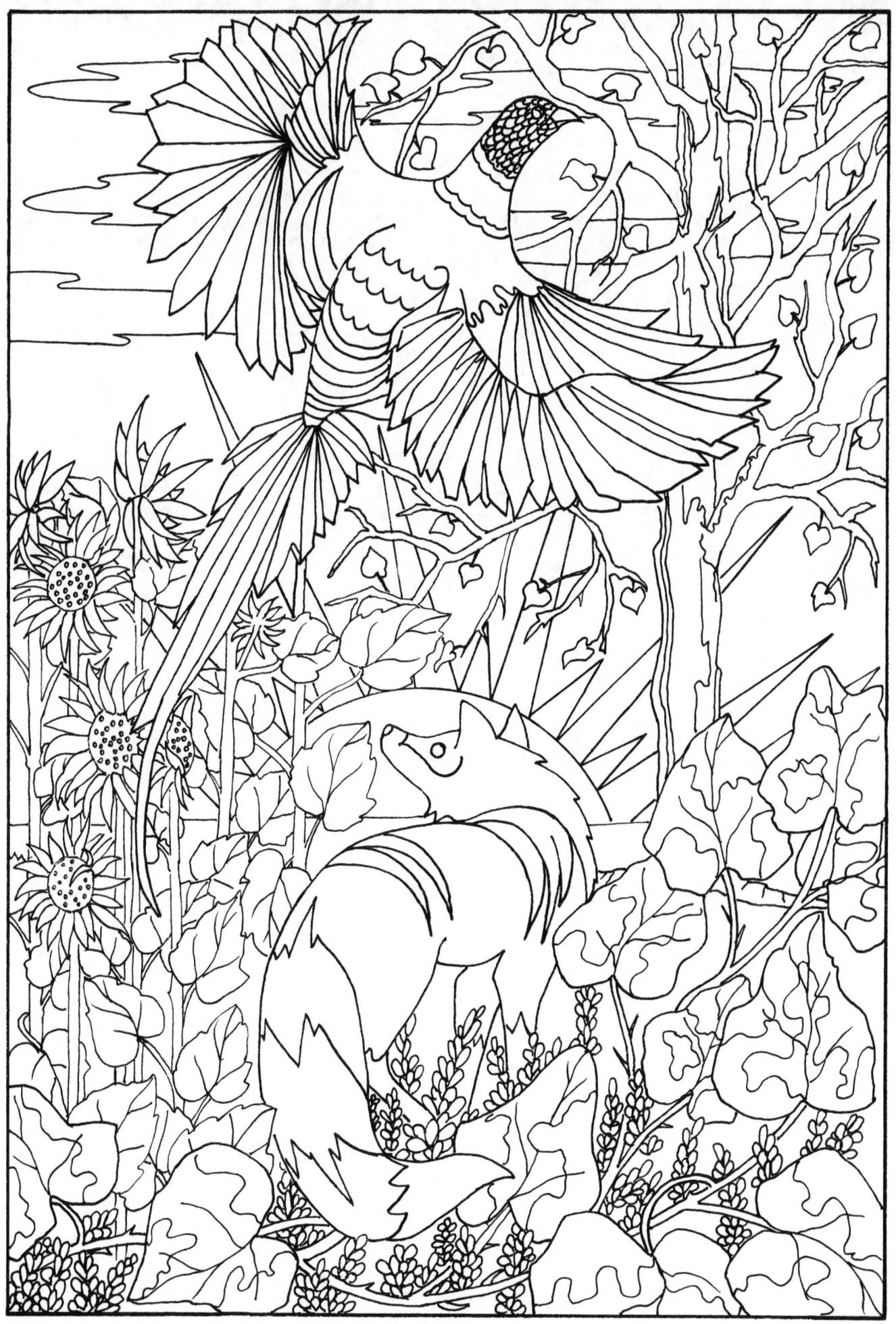

28. THE FOX AND THE PHEASANT

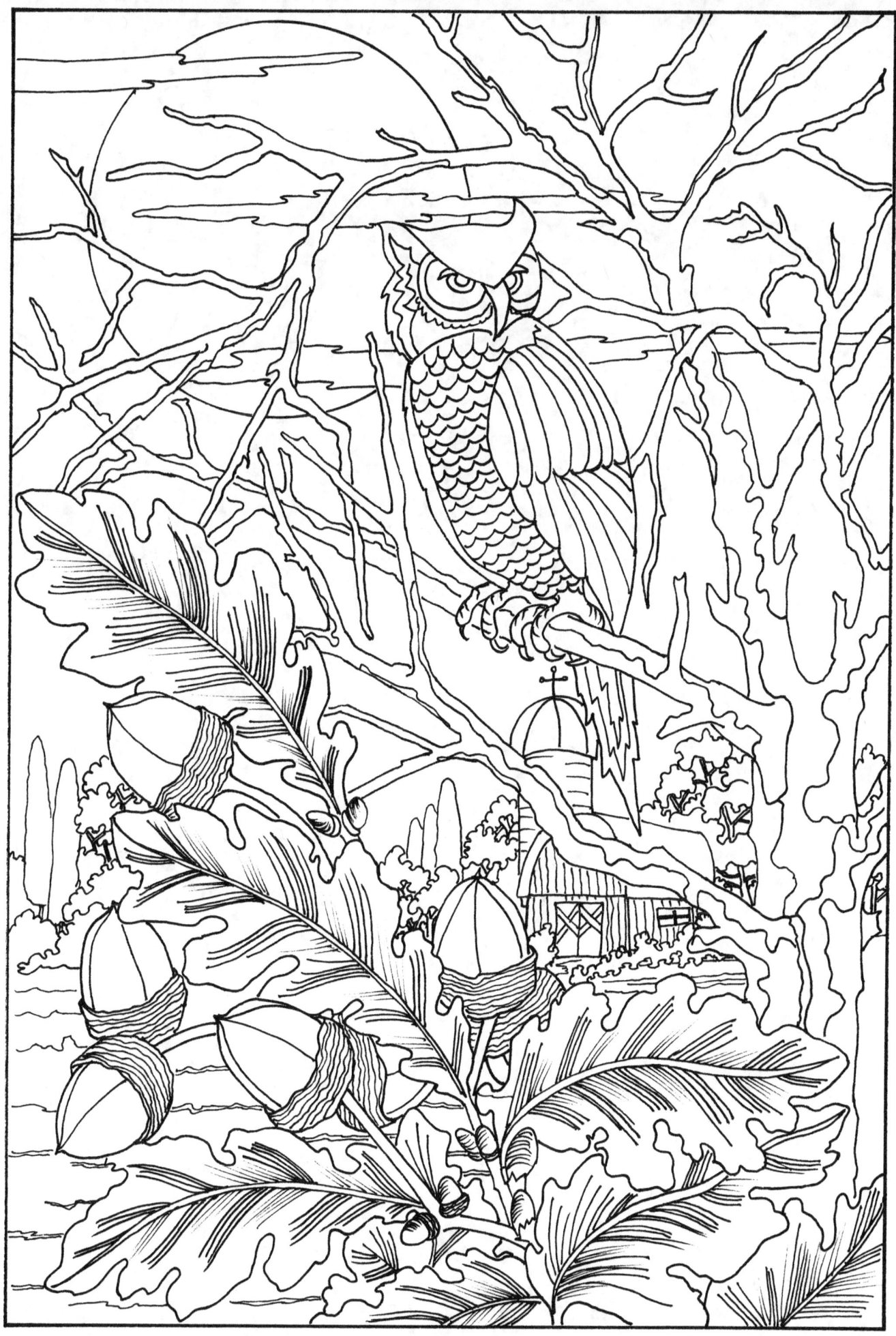

29. NIGHT OWL

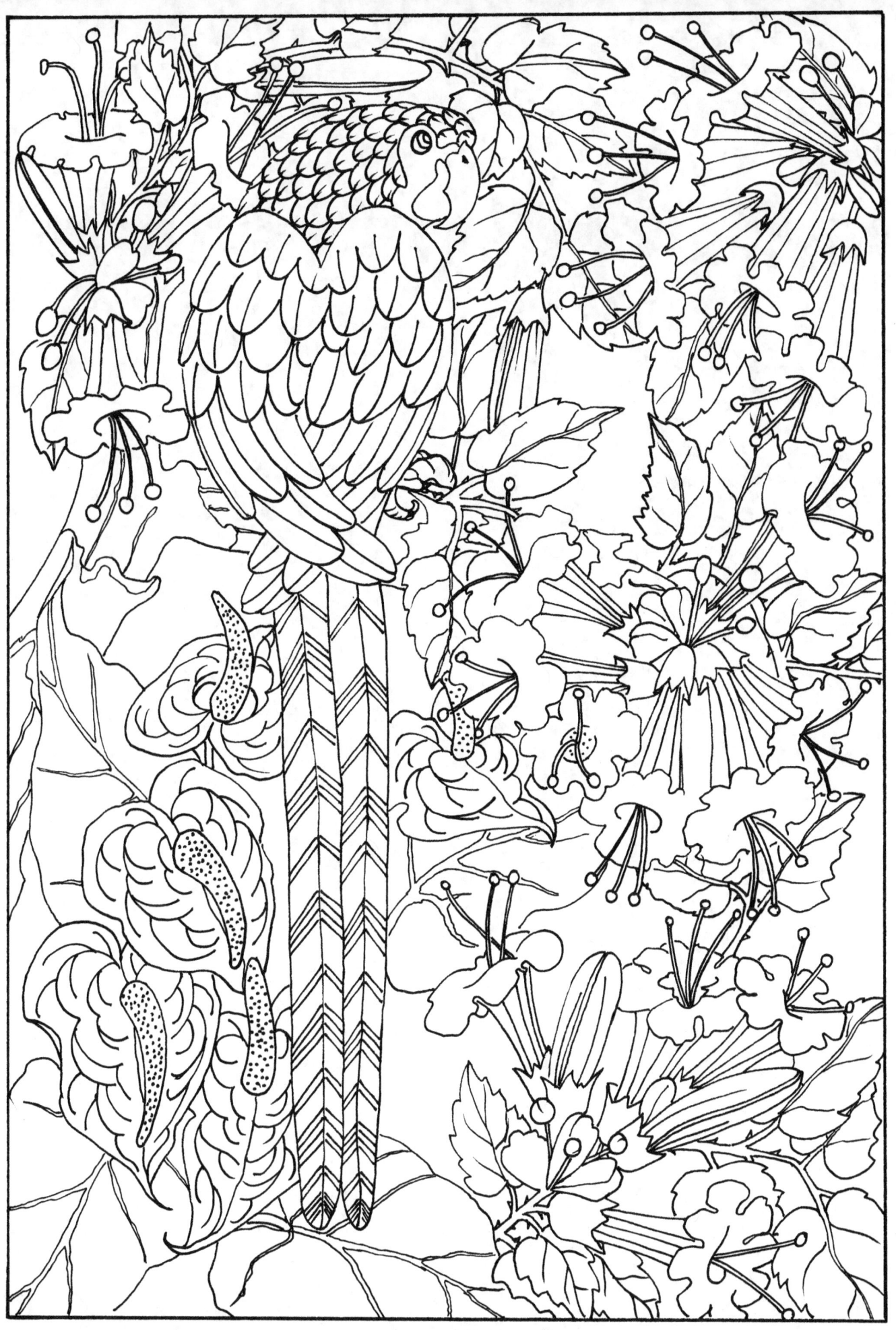

30. Macaw, Trumpet Vine, and Anthuriums

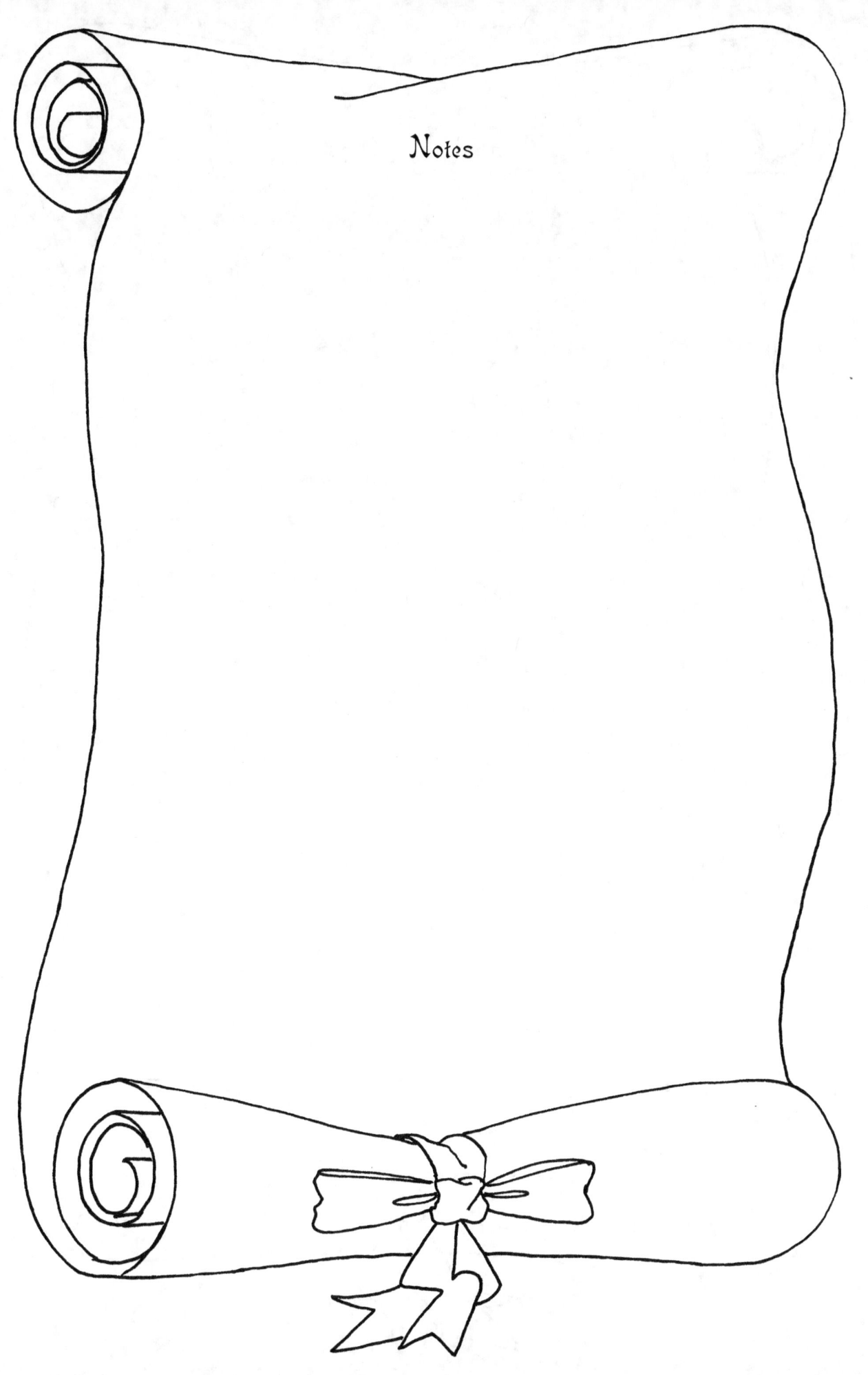

Notes

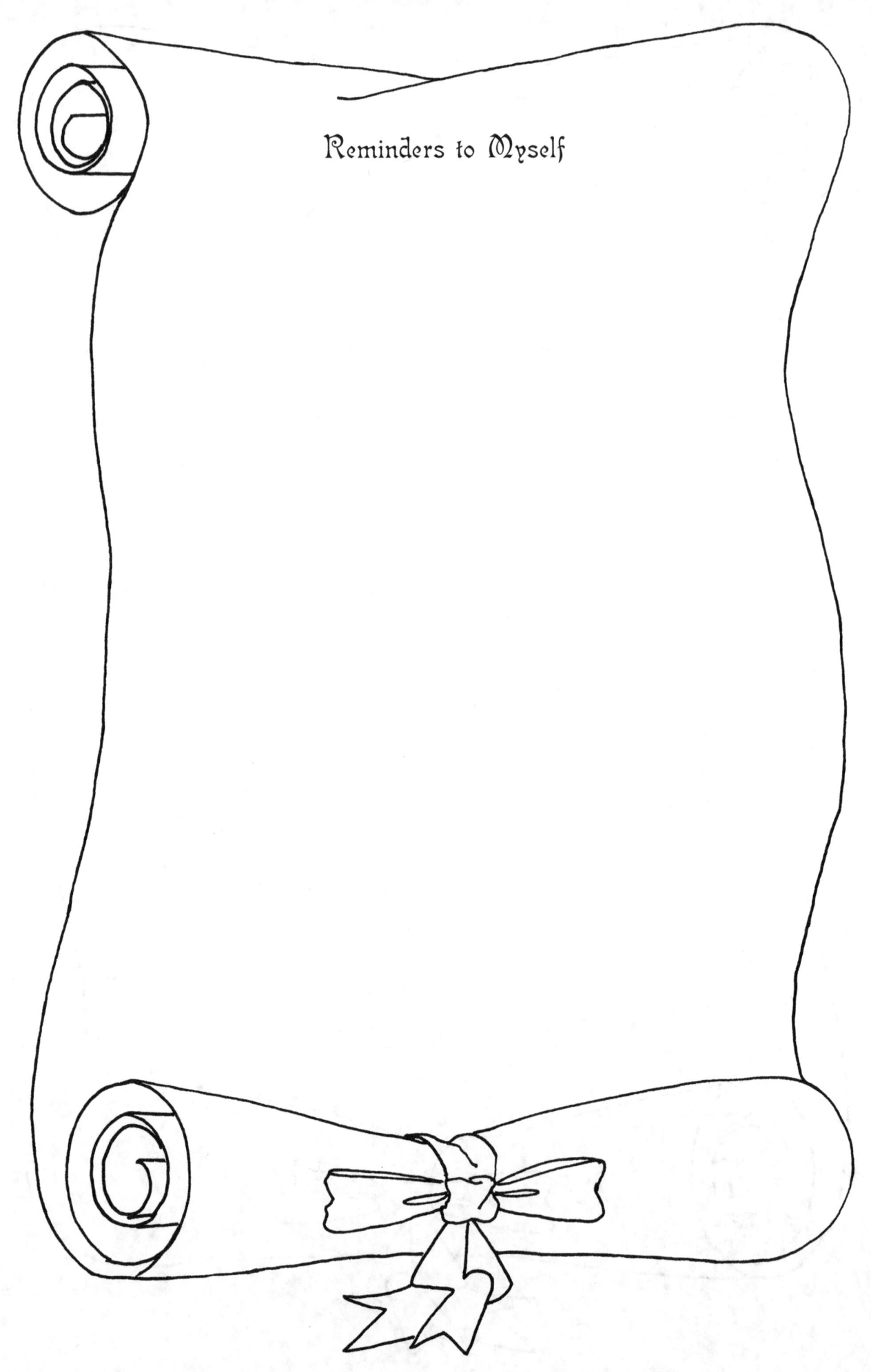

Reminders to Myself

www.ingramcontent.com/pod-product-compliance
Lightning Source LLC
Chambersburg PA
CBHW082014230526

45468CB00022B/2263